CITY IN TIME | **Chicago**

CITY IN TIME | Chicago

RAY FURSE

ORIGINAL PHOTOGRAPHY BY WERNHER KRUTEIN

STERLING

New York / London
www.sterlingpublishing.com

STERLING and the distinctive Sterling logo are registered trademarks of Sterling Publishing Co., Inc.

Library of Congress Cataloging-in-Publication Data

Furse, Ray.
    City in time. Chicago / Ray Furse.
        p. cm.
    ISBN-13: 978-1-4027-3299-7
    ISBN-10: 1-4027-3299-6
1. Chicago (Ill.)--History. 2. Chicago (Ill.)--Geography. 3. Chicago
(Ill.)—Pictorial works. 4. Historic buildings--Illinois--Chicago.
5.Chicago (Ill.)--Buildings, structures, etc.   I. Title. II. Title: Chicago.

F548.3.F88 2007
977.3'11--dc22

                                                        2006034468

10 9 8 7 6 5 4 3 2 1

Published by Sterling Publishing Co., Inc.
387 Park Avenue South, New York, NY 10016
© 2007 by Sterling Publishing Co., Inc.

Distributed in Canada by Sterling Publishing
c/o Canadian Manda Group, 165 Dufferin Street
Toronto, Ontario, Canada M6K 3H6
Distributed in the United Kingdom by GMC Distribution Services
Castle Place, 166 High Street, Lewes, East Sussex, England BN7 1XU
Distributed in Australia by Capricorn Link (Australia) Pty. Ltd.
P.O. Box 704, Windsor, NSW 2756, Australia

Design by 3+Co.

Sterling ISBN-13: 978-1-4027-3299-7
        ISBN-10: 1-4027-3299-6

For information about custom editions, special sales, premium and
corporate purchases, please contact Sterling Special Sales
Department at 800-805-5489 or specialsales@sterlingpub.com.

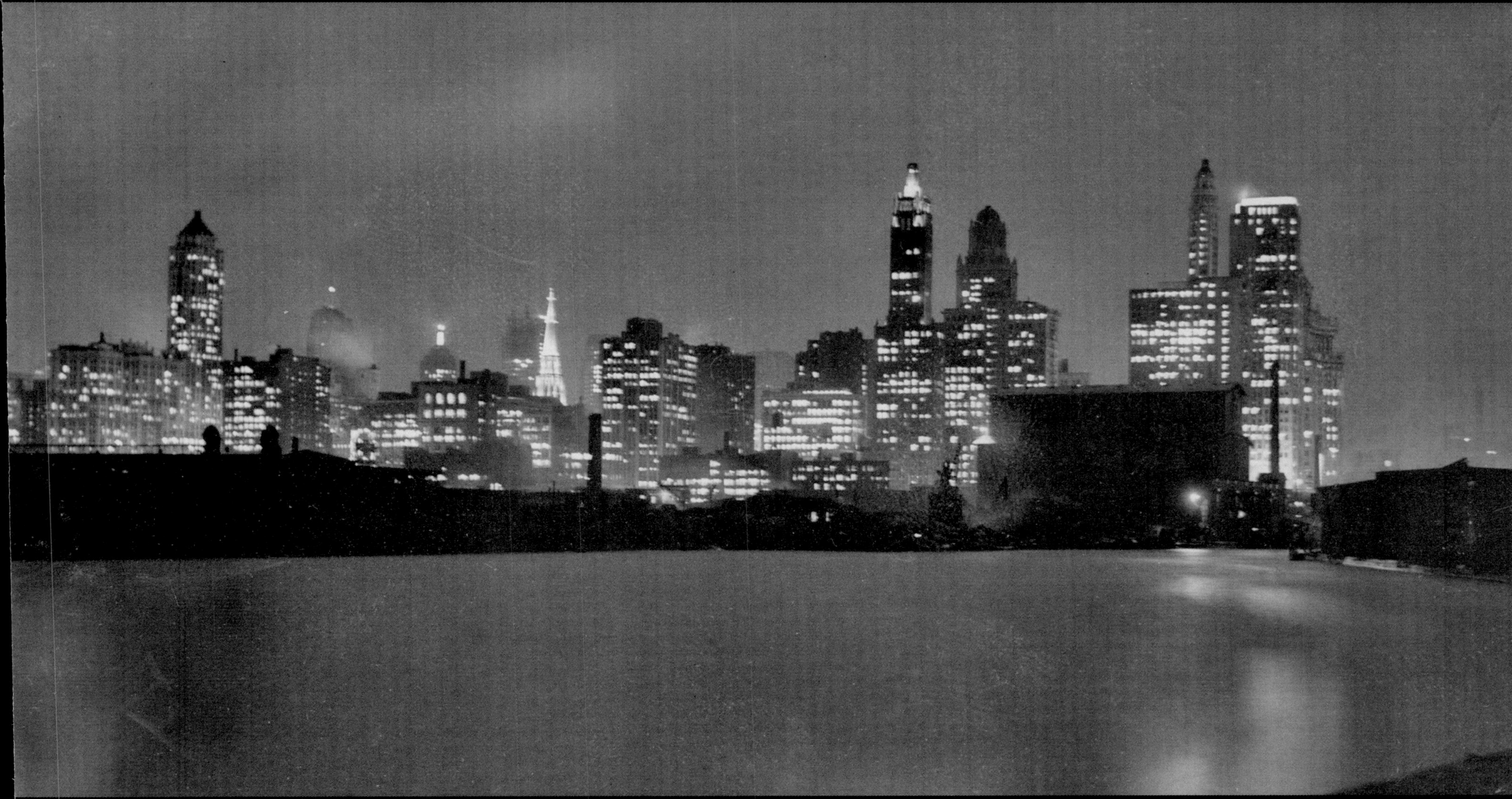

Preface

We hope that this volume of the City in Time series will compel you first to wonder at, then appreciate, and ulti-mately better understand the development and achievements of the world's great urban centers. The series offers not only interesting time-lapsed juxtapositions, but also meaningfully contrasting images that shed light on the unique resources, circumstances, and creative forces that propelled these cities to greatness. In a world where renovation and development are so often casually destructive, visual history can be a reservoir of wisdom from which we can inspire and refresh ourselves. We invite you to reflect upon the accomplishments of those who came before us and revel in these impressive monuments to human ambition.

Introduction

Make no little plans. They have no magic to stir men's blood and probably themselves will not be realized. Make big plans; aim high in hope and work, remembering that a noble, logical diagram once recorded will never die, but long after we are gone will be a living thing, asserting itself with ever-growing insistency. Remember that our sons and grandsons are going to do things that would stagger us. Let your watchword be order and your beacon beauty. Think big.

These famous words of Daniel Burnham (1846–1912), the great architect and city planner, reflect a mind-set that has always characterized Chicagoans. We may ascribe it to something in the prairie air or the waters of Lake Michigan, but ultimately we have to answer the question: How did a settlement founded in a pestilential swamp grow to become one of the world's greatest cities in just 200 years?

Of course, there were some obvious advantages to its success. It was positioned in the center of a vast and valuable swath of real estate called the Middle West, in a country that was expanding inexorably westward. It was surrounded by farmlands and forests that provided food and raw materials to fuel that growth. And it had ready access to the waterborne and, later, rail transportation that allowed it to service the growing enterprise that was America.

But other Midwestern towns—especially the more centrally located Kansas City and St. Louis on the great Mississippi—were equally well situated. There was something about Chicago that made it, in the words of Carl Sandburg's famous poem, "a tall bold slugger set vivid against the little soft cities."

Here came the great entrepreneurs: Sears, Roebuck, Montgomery Ward, and Marshall Field. A name perhaps less well known is that of Potter Palmer, who made millions in dry goods by declaring that "the customer is always right" and introducing "bargain days" (the first "sales"), money-back guarantees, and free home delivery. This man invented shopping.

Here came the great captains of industry and transport. McCormick's reaper may not excite today's technogroupies, but his company, which later became the giant International Harvester, revolutionized agriculture around the globe. Pullman's railroad cars made sure that the West could be won in style and comfort, while Mather's refrigerated railroad cars ensured that animals would arrive fresh to market. A restless and whimsical hive of inventiveness, Chicago gave the modern world zippers, Ferris wheels, and Twinkies. Oh, and let's not forget nuclear power.

And, finally, here came the great architects and builders, the Lords of the Skyscraper. See what Louis Sullivan could do with ironwork, what Ludwig Mies van der Rohe could do with glass and steel, what Frank Lloyd Wright could do with wood grains and rooflines. And see what Daniel Burnham could do with a city skyline.

Peruse these pages and you will be inspired, like Burnham, to think big.

CHICAGO

CHICAGO IN 1820
from Schiller Street North Side to 12th Street South Side.
The city extends beyond the souther line of 30th street given here; yet a distance of 2 miles to Egan Avenue (City limits) on the South Side and a distance of 1½ mile, beyond Schiller St to Fullerton Avenue on the North Side.
The entire length of the city from North to South being 7 Miles and breadth from East to West 3½ Miles.

IN 1868.

W here the Chicago River joins Lake Michigan has always been a natural depot for trade and transport. The Miami Indians, who were settled there in the early seventeenth century, named their village *Che-cau-gou* after the river, the word supposedly describing the smell of the wild onions that grew along its banks. The U.S. government acquired a tract of land for an outpost in 1795, and with the acquisition of the Louisiana Territory in 1803, exploring and defending Western Territories became more important. To this end, Fort Dearborn was constructed in 1803.

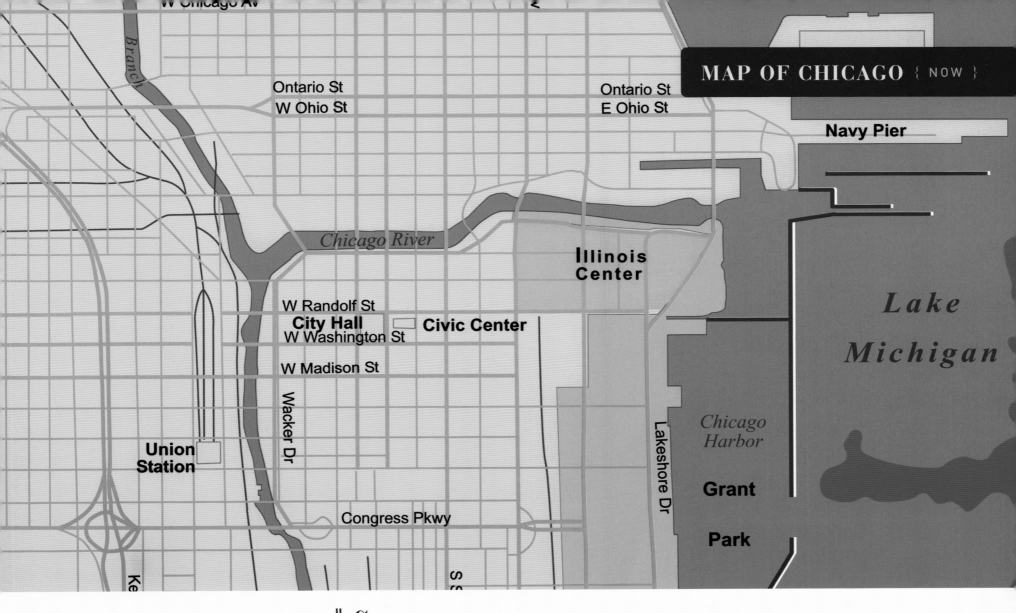

W Chicago Av

Ontario St
W Ohio St

Ontario St
E Ohio St

Navy Pier

Chicago River

Illinois Center

Lake Michigan

W Randolf St

City Hall
W Washington St

☐ **Civic Center**

W Madison St

Wacker Dr

Chicago Harbor

Union Station

Lakeshore Dr

Grant Park

Congress Pkwy

Branch

Ke

Chicago today covers 228 square miles with a population of approximately 3,000,000, making it the third most populous city in the nation. Nearly 10,000,000 people live in the greater metropolitan area, known informally and affectionately as Chicagoland. However, since its founding Chicago has had an influence extending far beyond its Midwestern location and relatively young age. It is ranked by the Globalization and World Cities Study Group & Network, for example, as one of 10 "Alpha" (most influential) cities in the world.

Chicago's success as an economic power has been due in no small measure to its location: at a point where the Chicago River meets Lake Michigan. Thus, Chicago grew as a great inland port, fortuitously situated where a vast network of Great Lakes waterways met a river system able to carry goods and passengers inland. The lakefront location is also responsible for deploying the city's amazing architecture along a north-south axis, resulting in Chicago's unobstructed and spectacular skyline.

It should come as no surprise then that Chicago's major north-south thoroughfare is called Lake Shore Drive and that the city's premier real estate is located along it. From the earliest days, however, efforts have been made to preserve the immediate lakefront from commercial development and to preserve its open spaces for public use. Today, the city's 29 miles of lakefront include 15 miles of bathing beaches, as well as public piers and marinas, and numerous parks with cultural attractions.

The earliest commitment on record to preserve the lakefront was made when Fort Dearborn, established in 1803 at the mouth of the Chicago River, began to outlive its usefulness. In discussing the dispensation of the land where the fort was located—a parcel acquired from Native Americans in 1795—it was vowed that part of it be kept for all time as "a public square, accessible at all times to the people."

In 1836, the Illinois legislature confirmed that forward-thinking view, mandating that much of the lakefront area be kept "forever open, clear and free." Although that did not prevent the Illinois Central Railroad yards from growing at the site, the lakefront has by and large, through many momentous struggles, been preserved for public uses. Looking south, one can see below the horizon (left to right) the Field Museum of Natural History and Soldier Field.

Prior to the 1830s, ships calling at Chicago had to anchor well offshore and transfer their cargo and passengers to small craft called "lighters" or "bateaux," which had drafts shallow enough to enter the Chicago River. In 1834, work was begun on cutting through a sandbar off the Lake Michigan shoreline to create a deeper, more useful harbor. By 1835, the *Illinois*—a 100-ton schooner—was able to enter the newly deepened river.

With the completion of the Illinois & Michigan Canal in 1848, the Chicago River became part of a direct water link between the Great Lakes and the Mississippi River. Grain, meat, lumber, stone, and finished goods went to their inland destinations east and west; as many as 288 boats worked the canal at its peak, transporting over a million tons in a single year. The city prospered as a major depot on a great thoroughfare supplying America's westward expansion. With that era long past, the boats you are most likely to see on the Chicago River today will be carrying tourists.

In 1867, a tunnel that extended two miles out into Lake Michigan—an engineering marvel of that time—was completed, addressing Chicago's increasing need for water due to its steadily growing population. A new pumping station designed by William W. Boyington was built at the intersection of Chicago and Michigan Avenues. Using limestone quarried in Joliet, Illinois, it incorporated Gothic architectural elements, with towers resembling a medieval castle. Most important, it could pump eighteen million gallons of water each day.

LORE & LEGEND

According to Dale Kaczmarek's *Windy City Ghosts*, one heroic worker stayed behind to man the pumps as the Great Chicago Fire of 1871 raged outside, finally choosing to hang himself in the tower rather than burn to death.

The central tower—located across Michigan Avenue from the pumping station and so readily recognized—was designed to hide a 138-foot standpipe needed to equalize pressure in the pipes. Completed in 1869, both the tower and pumping station were among the few structures to survive the Great Chicago Fire of 1871. Although newer pump designs eventually rendered such water towers obsolete and the standpipe was removed in 1911, the pumping station is still in use today, and both buildings are designated city landmarks.

A defining moment in Chicago city history came on October 8, 1871, when a fire broke out on DeKoven Street, supposedly in a barn owned by Catherine and Patrick O'Leary. Spreading to the north and driven by a gale-force wind, the Great Chicago Fire blazed for 36 hours, destroying three and a half square miles in the heart of the city. The fire leveled more than 18,000 structures, and at least 300 citizens perished.

LORE & LEGEND

Popular legend holds that a cow owned by Mrs. Catherine O'Leary kicked over a lantern, starting Chicago's Great Fire. However, the official inquiry exonerated Mrs. O'Leary and made no mention of a cow, suggesting that the story was made up after the fact.

CHICAGO FIRE ACADEMY

However, Chicagoans quickly began rebuilding, and most visible signs of the destruction were erased within a year. The Great Fire, in fact, confirmed Chicago's reputation as a place of renewal and opportunity. In May of 1971, a new Chicago Fire Academy was dedicated on the site where the Great Fire started. The $2.5-million complex is one of the most modern of such facilities in the country, and the more than 5,000 firefighters and paramedics of the Chicago Fire Department are among the world's best trained.

If there were no Chicago, there might be no . . .

FERRIS WHEEL

Bridge builder George W. Ferris built the first Ferris wheel, with a diameter of 250 feet, for the 1893 Chicago World's Fair in response to organizers wanting something that would rival the Eiffel Tower.

SOFTBALL

In November of 1887, indoor baseball was invented in Chicago, eventually to become softball due to its rather large (16 inches, later trimmed to 12 inches) and squishier ball.

MCDONALD'S

In 1955, the first McDonald's franchise restaurant, owned by Ray Kroc, opened in the Chicago suburb of Des Plaines.

SKYSCRAPERS

In 1889, the Chicago construction company of George A. Fuller completed the thirteen-story Tacoma Building, the first structure in which a riveted steel frame, rather than the walls, supported the building's weight.

STOCK CAR RACING

On Thanksgiving Day, 1895, the first auto race in the United States—which started at the Museum of Science and Industry, went to Evanston and then back to the museum—was won by Frank Duryea at an average speed of seven miles per hour.

ZIPPERS

Whitcomb Judson's "clasp locker" also first appeared at the 1893 Chicago World's Fair, although the name "zipper" did not become popular until much later.

TWINKIES

Bakery manager Jimmy Dewar invented this Depression-era treat made of golden sponge cake and banana filling. The filling was later changed to vanilla due to a wartime banana shortage.

NUCLEAR POWER

In 1942 the University of Chicago became the site of the world's first controlled and sustained atomic reaction.

BONE MARROW TRANSPLANTS

The first bone marrow transplant was performed at the University of Chicago in the late 1940s.

DAYTIME TV SOAPS

The first TV daytime soap opera, called These Are My Children, was broadcast from Chicago's NBC in 1949.

In 1874, a group of railroads agreed to jointly build a "Union Station" on the west side of the Chicago River. The station opened in 1881, but quickly became too small to handle Chicago's burgeoning growth. By the early decades of the twentieth century, Chicago was the undisputed rail center of the country. To accommodate the city's traffic of nearly 300 trains and 100,000 passengers daily, work on a new Union Station designed by the famed planner of public spaces Daniel Burnham began in 1913.

Labor and material shortages caused by World War I delayed the opening of the new Union Station until 1925. Although Burnham had died by then, the station was completed according to his plans and is considered one of the finest surviving monumental Beaux Arts passenger railroad stations. Its ornate main waiting room with a vaulted skylight 112 feet overhead is one of the nation's great interior public spaces. Union Station was designated a Chicago landmark in 2002 and is as busy as ever today; in 2006 approximately 126,000 people used the station daily.

At 292 feet wide and 3,000 feet long, this pier was the largest in the world when it opened to the public in 1916. Originally designated Municipal Pier Number 2, it offered shopping and recreation in addition to commercial port facilities. Renamed Navy Pier as a tribute to Navy personnel who served during World War I, it was also used by the Navy to train 15,000 pilots during World War II, among them a young airman named George Herbert Walker Bush.

LORE & LEGEND

As many as 200 World War II planes still rest at the bottom of Lake Michigan as a result of accidents during pilot training.

At its peak in 1964, Navy Pier was handling 250 overseas vessels annually and was one of the greatest inland ports in the world. During the 1970s, it fell into disuse but was resurrected decades later through a $150 million redevelopment project. By 1995 the pier was reborn, and today it features a mix of year-round entertainment, shops, restaurants, attractions, and exhibition facilities.

Foremost among Chicago's famous merchant names are those of Richard Warren Sears and Alvah Roebuck. Founded in 1893, their company achieved instant success through mail-order catalog sales that reached rural customers. But as urban populations grew, Sears, Roebuck joined the trend toward building large downtown stores; the State Street store (above) was one of 27 opened between 1925 and 1927. Although competition and poor business drove Sears from State Street in the 1980s, it returned in 2001, only to a different location.

LORE & LEGEND

Consumers had such trust in Sears mail-order products that, in 1908, the company began offering entire houses in kits called Sears Modern Homes. By the time the program ended in 1940, more than 100,000 kits had been sold.

LORE & LEGEND

The Sears Tower was scaled in August of 1999 by French urban climber Alain "Spiderman" Robert. Unannounced and using no safety devices, he climbed the exterior glass and steel wall to the top using only his bare hands and feet.

Completed in 1973, the Sears Tower was built as the corporate headquarters for the diversified retail chain. It was the tallest building in the world at the time, rising to 1,454 feet (including antennas), and is currently the tallest building in North America. Sears, Roebuck no longer owns it, though. Although it was the largest retailer in the United States until the early 1980s, Sears was buffeted by competition and was purchased by rival Kmart in 2004. The new corporation continues to operate stores under both brands.

BUCKINGHAM FOUNTAIN { THEN }

On the evening of October 21, 1929, Henry Ford hosted an elaborate celebration in Dearborn, Michigan, to honor his friend Thomas A. Edison, who had invented the electric light fifty years earlier. The event was known as Light's Golden Jubilee, and a huge publicity campaign encouraged the entire world to join in. People waited in the dark and listened to the radio reporting as Edison reenacted his earlier success. On cue, switches were thrown to bathe the world in light, including enthusiastic crowds at Buckingham Fountain in Grant Park.

With 134 jets sending 14,000 gallons of water skyward to heights of 150 feet each minute, Buckingham Fountain is one of the largest fountains in the world. Officially the Clarence Buckingham Memorial Fountain, it was modeled after the Bassin de Latome fountain at Versailles and donated to the city in 1927 by Kate Buckingham in memory of her brother. Today it remains a favored Chicago landmark, with crowds gathering every evening to see its 820 lights and aquatic display set to music.

Although there is some dispute about precisely which building constituted the world's first "skyscraper"—a building that is supported by its frame, rather than its walls—there is no argument that it was located in Chicago. Some architectural historians cite the first as the 10-story Home Insurance Building (1885), which featured a fireproof metal skeleton. Others claim it was the 13-story Tacoma Building (1889), the first structure to use a riveted steel frame.

Courtesy of Skidmore, Owings & Merrill LLP

LORE & LEGEND

Interviewed for Chicago's WGN television on September 23, 2003, Donald Trump revealed that "Prior to September 11, we had plans for a building of approximately 150 stories."

Today Chicago boasts a fleet of mega towers to rival any city in the world. The latest (scheduled for completion in 2008), tallest (92 stories reaching 1,131 feet), and costliest ($750 million) of these is Trump International Hotel and Tower, built on the site of the dilapidated Sun Times Building. The tower design blends well with its several majestic neighbors. Its first setback is at the same height as the cornice on the Wrigley Building; the second is the same height as Marina City; and the third matches the top of the IBM Building across the street.

Although Chicago's Lyric Opera is world renown today, opera in Chicago was slow in getting started and encountered one setback after another. When a small opera troupe first arrived in 1850, the theater in which it was performing burned down on the second night. Fifteen years later impresario Uranus Crosby used his considerable fortune—amassed distilling whisky during the Civil War—to open Crosby's Opera House, which showcased touring opera companies until it also burned down in the Great Fire of 1871.

LORE & LEGEND

Uranus Crosby's grand opera house had to wait for its opening-day celebration in 1865 because of the assassination of Abraham Lincoln. Within a year, Crosby realized the endeavor would be a continuing financial burden, so he

organized a lottery to get rid of it. Buyers could take a chance on owning it for the price of a $5 ticket. Celebration of a lavish renovation in 1871 was scheduled on the first full day of the Great Fire, when it burned to the ground.

In 1929 the city's second permanent resident company, the Chicago Civic Opera, moved into the lavish new Civic Opera House. This 45–story mix of Art Nouveau and Art Deco styles featured a beautiful auditorium with excellent sight lines and acoustics. Unfortunately, the move came just six days after the stock market crash, and the opera company closed shortly thereafter. Opera was reborn in Chicago with the creation of the Lyric Opera in 1952, with its permanent home in the now completely restored Civic Opera Building.

In October of 1871, the two Catholic churches of Chicago were destroyed when the Great Fire engulfed the city. Church of the Holy Name pastor John McMullen traveled the country to raise funds to rebuild both churches and to help the city's homeless. For more than four years, Chicago's Catholics worshipped in what was called the "shanty cathedral," a burned and boarded-up house on Cass Street.

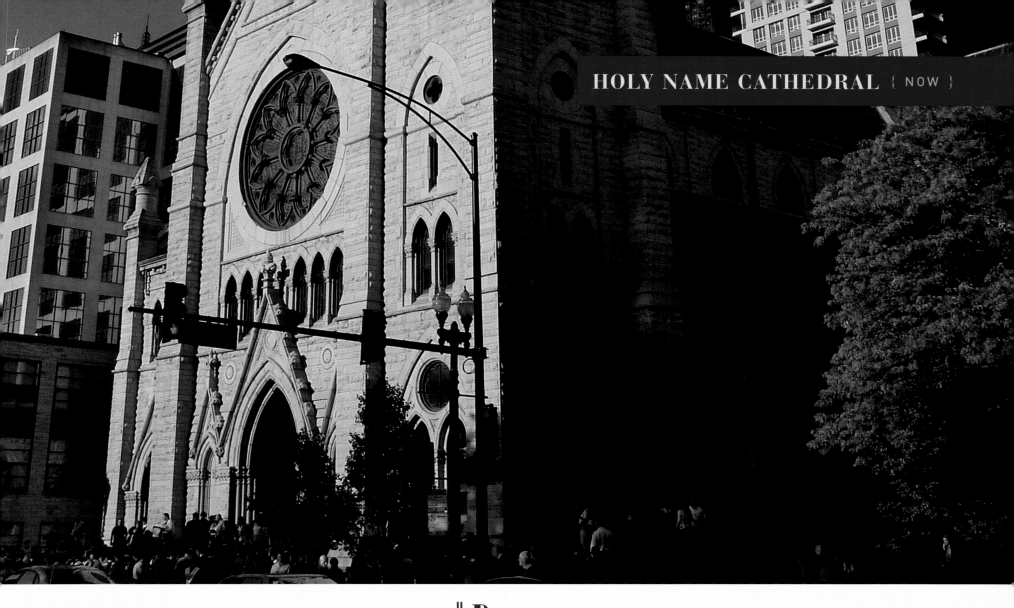

Dedicated on November 21, 1875, Holy Name Cathedral, formally the Church of the Holy Name, sits on the corner of North State Street at Superior Street. The seat of the Roman Catholic Archdiocese of Chicago, it is a gorgeous example of Gothic-style architecture and one of the busiest parishes in the city. The church building is 233 feet long, 126 feet wide, and can seat 1,520 people. The ceiling is 70 feet high and has a spire that reaches upward to 210 feet.

Although noted as an enclave of geniuses rather than jocks, the University of Chicago was an original member of the Big Ten Conference and a football powerhouse for many years. Home games were played at Marshall Field, donated by the eponymous Chicago merchant. The name was later changed to Stagg Field in honor of Amos Alonzo Stagg, head football coach at the university for 41 years. The university discontinued intercollegiate football after 1939, and it was not reinstituted at the varsity level until 1969.

LORE & LEGEND

On December 2, 1942, in the handball courts beneath the abandoned west bleachers of Stagg Field, a team of scientists led by Enrico Fermi built an "atomic pile," achieving

REGENSTEIN LIBRARY { NOW }

the first self-sustaining nuclear chain reaction and paving the way for the development of atomic power and the atomic bomb.

ocated east of Ellis Avenue and north of 57th Street, the old 50,000-seat Stagg Field was eventually torn down and reestablished on a more modest scale just to the northwest. The Regenstein Library was built on the original Stagg Field site and opened in 1970. Housing more than 6,000,000 volumes and 7,000,000 other documents on seven levels (two underground), "the Reg" is considered to be among the top five libraries in the world for the breadth and depth of its holdings.

You've "visited" Chicago if you've seen:

- ABOUT LAST NIGHT...
  (1986)

- ADVENTURES
  IN BABYSITTING
  (1987)

- A LEAGUE OF THEIR OWN
  (1992)

- BAD BOYS
  (1995)

- FERRIS BUELLER'S DAY OFF
  (1986)

- HOME ALONE I, II, or III
  (1990, 1992, 1997)

- NATIONAL LAMPOON'S
  CHRISTMAS VACATION
  (1989)

- OCEAN'S 11 or OCEAN'S 12
  (2001, 2004)

- RISKY BUSINESS
  (1983)

- SIXTEEN CANDLES
  (1984)

- THE BLUES BROTHERS
  (1980)

- THE BREAKFAST CLUB
  (1985)

- THE COLOR OF MONEY
  (1986)

- THE FUGITIVE
  (1993)

- THE UNTOUCHABLES
  (1987)

- UNCLE BUCK
  (1989)

- WHEN HARRY MET SALLY...
  (1989)

- WEIRD SCIENCE
  (1985)

- WHAT WOMEN WANT
  (2000)

and, of course,

- CHICAGO
  (2002)

Founded in 1875 by Melville H. Stone, the upstart *Chicago Daily News* published the city's first one-cent newspaper, an afternoon edition; in 1881, it introduced a two-cent morning edition. Its competition was the more patrician *Chicago Tribune*, founded in 1847 and selling for a nickel a copy. By 1903, when this photo of its West Wells office was taken, the *Daily News* was the city's most popular paper, remaining so until 1918, when the circulation crown was reclaimed by the *Tribune*.

The *Chicago Daily News* remained an important newspaper, however, and moved into a splendid, 26-floor Art Deco headquarters at 400 West Madison Street in 1929. With more than 2,000 employees, the paper enjoyed a circulation of about 430,000. But media competition became increasingly intense, and the paper ceased to exist in 1978. Fortunately, its rich collection of more than 55,000 images of urban Chicago life captured on glass plate negatives between 1902 and 1933 were preserved; most of the historical images in this book were drawn from that collection.

One of America's great merchandising pioneers, Marshall Field was born in 1834 on a Massachusetts farm and headed to Chicago at age 21 to seek his fortune. The great emporium he created catered to urban women with leisure time. Rather than "Buyer beware," Field's motto was "Give the lady what she wants." Store amenities included restaurants, lounges, a library, a nursery, and telephones. Ladies could check their coats, write letters on complimentary Marshall Field's stationery, and even hold meetings there.

LORE & LEGEND

Marshall Field's is also famous for its mouthwatering chocolate-covered Frango Mints, first offered in their store in 1929. In 1999 Marshall Field's decided to shift production from its store to a Pennsylvania candy maker.

Frangophiles were outraged when they heard the news. The protest was quelled somewhat by the disclosure that Frango mints are still produced where they were actually invented—Seattle.

Hovering 18 feet above the sidewalk and weighing nearly eight tons, the clock at Marshall Field's was installed at the corner of Washington and State Streets in November of 1897. A 1907 rebuilding and expansion resulted in today's store, which covers an entire city block with its seven stories in the Neoclassical style. Both clock and store have served as symbols of Chicago and familiar meeting places for more than a century. In 2006, following its acquisition by Federated Department Stores, the Marshall Field's name was changed to Macy's.

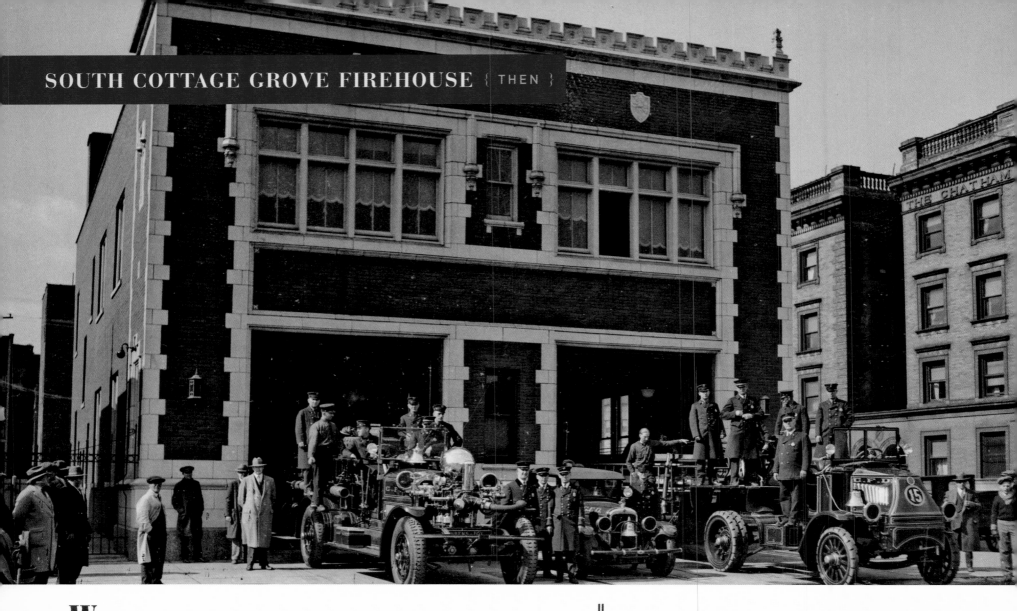

W hen Chicago was incorporated in 1833, its firefighters were all volunteers. The first firehouse, with two hand-pump engines, was on LaSalle Street where City Hall now stands. The first paid fire department was organized 1858, and over the years many new stations were added; when this brick station house opened on South Cottage Grove Avenue in 1928, its firefighting crew proudly arrayed its equipment out front for a newspaper photo.

An 1835 city ordinance required every city resident or owner "to have one good painted leather fire-bucket, with the initials of the owner's name painted thereon" hung within reach of each fireplace or stove. Steam-drive pumps replaced hand pumps after 1858, although hose carts were still pulled by men running at top speed, with the engines drawn by horses. The first fire-alarm boxes were installed in 1865, and the fire department stopped using horses to pull its trucks in 1923, just five years before this station first opened.

Chicago had no public library when, prior to his death in 1868, Walter Loomis Newberry drew up a will providing for one to be established in the northern section of the city. Newberry had made his fortune in banking, shipping, and real estate, and was an active book collector, founder of the Young Men's Library Association, and president of the Chicago Historical Society. The present building, designed by the Newberry's first librarian, William Frederick Poole, and architect Henry Ives Cobb, opened in 1893 on West Walton Street.

LORE & LEGEND

The Newberry is located at "Bughouse Square" (from "bughouse," slang for a mental health facility) the popular name of Washington Square Park. In the 1920s and '30s,

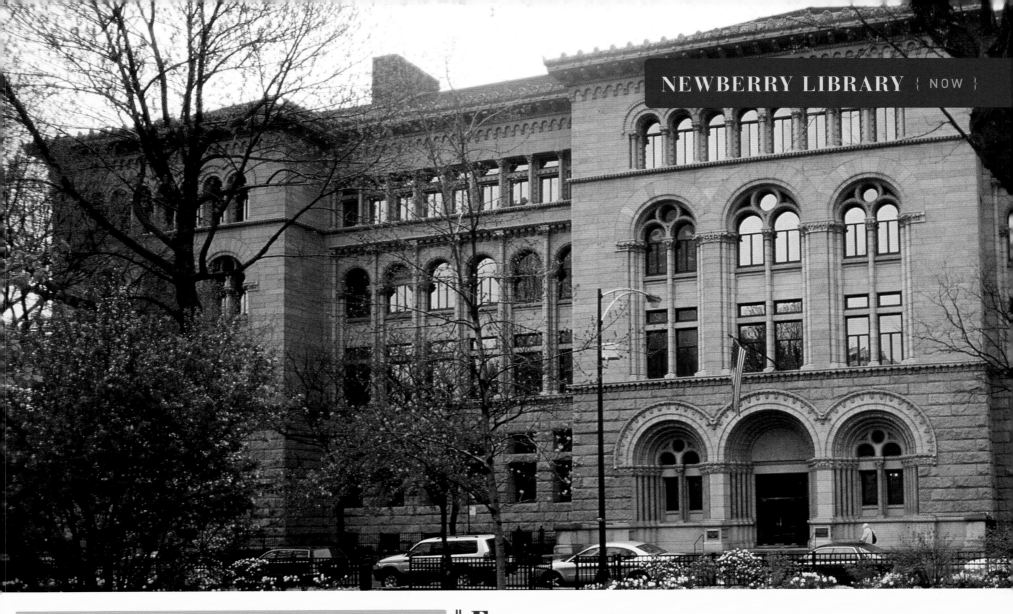

this was the favored spot for poets, preachers, revolutionary leftists, and crackpots who harangued the crowds.

Free and open to the public, the Newberry remains an independent research library and educational institution. The collections number 1,500,000 printed titles, 5,000,000 manuscript pages, and 300,000 historic maps relating to the European discovery, exploration, and settlement of the Americas (including Latin America), and French and British history and literature. Specialized collections focus on such diverse topics as North American Indians, the history of cartography, the history and theory of music, and the history of printing.

The first baseball park on Chicago's North Side was built in 1914 by Charlie Weeghman for his Chicago Federals team. When their league folded in 1916, Weeghman purchased the National League Cubs with other investors, among them chewing gum magnate William Wrigley Jr., who later bought out his partners. Wrigley Field is a source of much baseball tradition; the custom of allowing fans to keep foul balls hit into the stands started here, as did the custom of throwing back homers hit by opposing players.

LORE & LEGEND

The Cubs have never won a World Series title at Wrigley, having lost in all six attempts since 1918. Their last world championship came in 1908, six years before Wrigley was built.

LORE & LEGEND

Wind conditions affect play at Wrigley Field more than at any other major league park. Winds from Lake Michigan favor pitchers, but winds blowing toward the lake can loft home runs.

Beloved by baseball fans, Wrigley featured an ivy-covered outfield wall and a grass field long after other stadiums had upgraded to dome-covered Astroturf. The first permanent concession stand in baseball was built here in 1914. In 1937, a 75-foot-wide scoreboard rising was installed—it is still manually operated. Wrigley was for many years the only major stadium without lights, and games that ran into darkness were simply called off. After 5,687 consecutive day games played by the Cubs at Wrigley, lights were installed, and the first night game was played in 1988.

At the turn of the last century, the corner of Washington and Dearborn Streets in the Loop area housed a sleepy cigar store. Today the Richard J. Daley Center stands here, named after the mayor who in 1966 dedicated the $87-million building as the Civic Center; it was renamed in his honor after he died in office in 1976. The exterior of the award-winning building is constructed of glass and a special steel alloy responsible for the permanent russet-colored oxide coating.

Pablo Picasso was entreated by architect William Hartmann to produce a model for a monumental sculpture to be installed in the Civic Center's plaza. Picasso not only agreed, but also refused a fee for his work, preferring to give the work as a "gift to the people of Chicago," a place he had never visited. Executed by the United States Steel Corporation from Picasso's 42-inch steel model, the finished sculpture (far right)—standing 50 feet high and weighing 162 tons—is made of the same type of steel as the exterior of the building.

Potter Palmer (1826–1902) operated a successful dry-goods store in partnership with Marshall Field until he sold his interest to speculate in real estate. He acquired a three-quarter-mile stretch of State Street and began development of the property, opening the first Palmer House Hotel in 1870. A second was under construction when all of his State Street properties were destroyed in the Great Fire of 1871. He borrowed money and began rebuilding; the third incarnation of the Palmer House Hotel (shown above) opened in 1875 and featured a separate ladies' entrance.

LORE & LEGEND

The 1875 Palmer House Hotel was so sumptuous that it was both praised and mocked. Rudyard Kipling described it as "a gilded and mirrored rabbit-warren. crammed with people talking about money and spitting about everywhere."

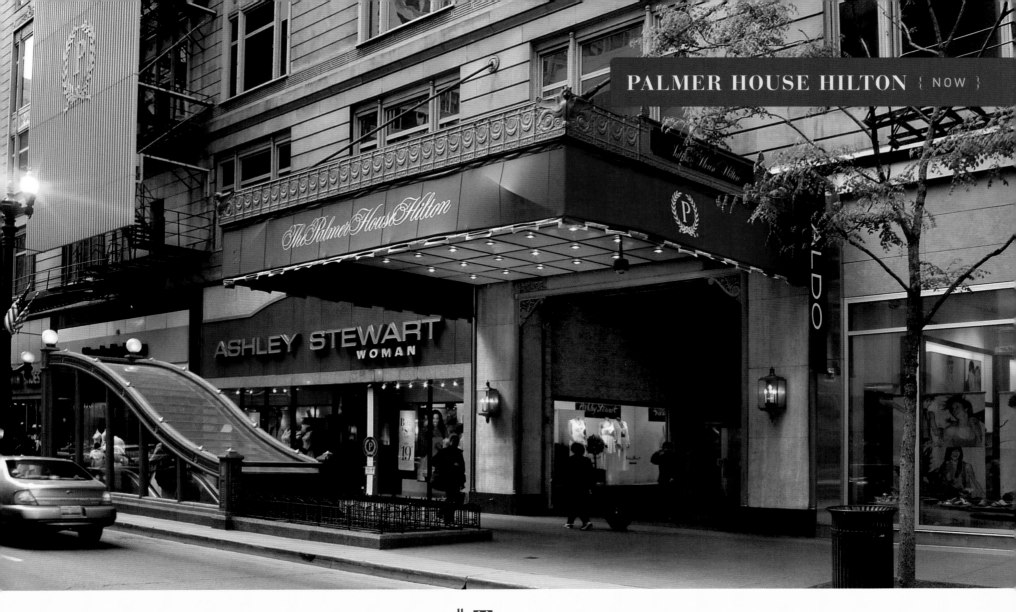

The 1875 Palmer House was even more lavish than its predecessors, featuring Italian marble and elaborate mosaics, while the floor of the barbershop was tiled with silver dollars. Its amenities included oversized rooms, luxurious decor, and sumptuous meals served in grand style. Advertised as the nation's only fireproof hotel, it was replaced in 1925 by the modern, multitowered 25-story structure (above), now a member of the Hilton chain and still quite luxurious.

Named after hotelmen John and Tracy Drake, this longtime rival of the Palmer House was constructed of smooth limestone in Italian Renaissance–style on what was then a Lake Michigan landfill. Even before The Drake Hotel opened in 1920, *The Economist* reported that it would be "of unusual magnificence, nothing like it in appearance, arrangement or finishing having ever been attempted in this country." Although the Drakes lost ownership during the Great Depression, the family name has been retained.

LORE & LEGEND

Among the powerful and famous The Drake has hosted are Emperor Hirohito, Queen Elizabeth II, Prince Phillip, and Princess Diana, King Hussein, Jawaharlal Nehru,

Winston Churchill, Eleanor Roosevelt, Presidents Hoover, Eisenhower, Ford, Reagan, and celebrities such as Charles Lindbergh, Walt Disney, and Elizabeth Taylor.

The Drake has many rooms of architectural note, such as the Ballroom, the French Room, and the private Club International, the latter a reproduction of Haddon Hall, a notable example of a medieval residence in Derbyshire, England. From the lavish Gold Coast Room, the music of the fabulous big bands of that era was broadcast live by WGN, whose studios were located in The Drake. The Drake has been listed on the National Register of Historic Places, joining such other Chicago landmarks as Louis Sullivan's Carson Pirie Scott building and the old Water Tower.

Certainly America's most famous architect, Frank Lloyd Wright (1867–1959) is responsible for reshaping American ideas about residential architecture in the twentieth century. His inspiration for an indigenous style had its roots in the flat and expansive landscape of the American Midwest, where he was born and grew up. Hence, Wright's "Prairie style" emphasized, in his own words, "gently sloping roofs, low proportions, quiet sky lines . . . sheltering overhangs, low terraces and out-reaching walls sequestering private gardens."

LORE & LEGEND

It is said that, while working under the great architect Louis H. Sullivan, Frank Lloyd Wright learned to devise creative architectural solutions rather than simply rely upon the accepted conventions of the day. One convention he flouted

was the firm's policy against moonlighting. When Sullivan discovered his employee working on projects outside the firm, he fired Wright, who then started his own architectural business in 1893.

From 1889 to 1909, Wright lived and worked in his home and studio at 951 Chicago Avenue, in the suburb of Oak Park. He used his home as an architectural laboratory, experimenting with design concepts that developed into a coherent architectural philosophy. Here he raised six children with his first wife, Catherine Tobin, and designed 125 structures with his associates. Of the more than 300 Wright-designed buildings constructed, more than 100 are in the Chicago metropolitan area.

Chicagoland Food

If Chicago gets an "A" for it's culinary contributions, it would have to stand for abundance. Chicagoans work hard, play harder, and eat heartily. Consider the two most famous food items with documented roots in Chicago: the hot dog and deep-dish pizza.

THE CHICAGO HOT DOG

In 1929, the Great Depression created a demand for both jobs and good cheap food, so greengrocer Abe Drexler converted his vegetable cart on Maxwell street into a hot-dog stand. There, his son Jake "Fluky" Drexler sold a glorified, veggie-covered dog called the "Depression Sandwich" for a nickel each. It was an instant success, and the Chicago Hot Dog was born.

Today you can try a Chicago Hot Dog at any of approximately 2,000 locations. Purists insist that you must use an all beef—preferably Vienna-brand— frankfurter, steamed and placed in a poppy-seed bun. But it's really the toppings that make a Chicago Hot Dog. These must be added, according to traditionalists, in this order: yellow mustard; sweet pickle relish; chopped onions; chopped or sliced tomatoes; kosher dill-pickle spears; hot green peppers; and celery salt. Beware: asking for ketchup is as gross a culinary faux pas that is along the same lines as asking for mayonnaise on your corned beef at a Jewish deli.

Chicago's Pizzeria Uno claims that the first deep-dish pizza was created at its original location in 1943, supposedly by a Texan named Ike Sewell. It was so popular that business thrived and a Pizzeria Due was opened up nearby. The demand for the dish is attributed to the fact that it presented pizza—soon to explode in popularity due to returning GIs who had tasted it in Italy—with the ease and bounty of the casserole, which had great appeal to Midwestern American tastes.

Today there are more than 2,000 pizzerias in Chicago. The deep-dish style is much more like a casserole than its thin-crusted Italian ancestor, but that makes it easy to create. In a deep dish lined with pizza dough, pile mozzarella cheese; coarsely crushed plum tomatoes; chopped fresh garlic, basil, and oregano. The whole is topped with grated Parmesan cheese. Free to add: crumbled Italian sausage, hot or sweet; sliced pepperoni; sliced yellow onions, mushrooms, green peppers, and black olives.

"Settlement houses" first arose in London in the 1880s as a response to social problems created by urbanization and immigration; they typically attracted native-born, educated, middle-class women and men to become involved ("settle") in the life of poor urban neighborhoods. Hull House was opened by Jane Addams in 1889 in the Charles Hull mansion on South Halsted street. Aided by a committed staff, Miss Addams helped hundreds of immigrants and the poor gain a place of self-respect in society.

Over the years, a dozen other buildings were added to form a two-city-block complex with rooms for English and citizenship classes, club meetings, a nursery school, day care, the only library and art gallery in the area, and one of the first gymnasiums in the country. For her work promoting peace and social justice, Jane Addams won the Nobel Peace Prize in 1931. Although most of the Hull House complex has since been leveled, the remaining two buildings—declared a National Historic Landmark in June of 1967—house the Jane Addams Hull House Museum.

Standing on the most prestigious real estate in the city—where Michigan Avenue crosses the Chicago River—are two of Chicago's most noted architectural monuments, the Wrigley Building and the Tribune Tower. Built in 1920, the Wrigley Building (left), headquarters of the chewing gum company, stands out because of its sparkling white terra-cotta and well-proportioned architecture modeled after the Giralda Tower of Seville Cathedral. Its giant two-story tower clock, which is floodlit at night, has helped make it a Chicago icon.

LORE & LEGEND

The Tribune Tower has stones from famous sites embedded in its walls and on view, including a moon rock, fragments from the Alamo, the Roman Coliseum, the Great Pyramid of Cheops, the Great Wall of China, and many others.

In 1922 a design competition for a new headquarters of the *Chicago Daily Tribune* was won by Raymond Hood—who would later build Rockefeller Center in New York—and John Howell. Their Gothic design (right), modeled after the Button Tower of the Rouen Cathedral in France, was criticized at the time, as it went against the modernizing trend set by the Chicago School and the more functional International Style becoming popular in Europe. Nonetheless, the Tribune Tower, decorative buttresses and all, was completed in 1925 and remains a Chicago favorite.

When retired Sears, Roebuck and Co. vice president Max Adler toured Europe in 1928, he visited a number of the new domed theaters in which the night sky was projected above the audience. Nearly a dozen European cities boasted these new "planetariums," made possible by the new Mark II "planetarium projectors" invented by Carl Zeiss Optics. A philanthropist with an interest in science, Adler believed not only that Chicago should have such a facility but also that the city could build a better one.

The Adler Planetarium opened in May 1930, incorporating a Mark II projector, which was donated by Max Adler along with money to build the landmark 12-sided theater that houses it. Designed by Ernst Grunsfeld, it was the first modern planetarium in the western hemisphere and is the oldest in existence today. The expanded and completely renovated facilities now house the original Zeiss planetarium theater and the StarRider theater, offering a computer-simulated virtual ride through the universe. The Adler also contains more than 35,000 square feet of exhibits, including historical astronomical instruments and rare books on astronomy.

Opened in 1930, the Merchandise Mart was constructed by retail magnate Marshall Field; it was designed in the Art Deco–style by the firm of Graham, Anderson, Probst and White, responsible for such other Chicago monuments as the Field Museum, Union Station, the Museum of Science and Industry, the Civic Opera Building, and the Wrigley Building. The enormous structure spans two entire city blocks and rises 25 stories, encompassing 4.2 million square feet. It even has its own station on the Chicago Transit Authority's "L" system.

LORE & LEGEND

The Merchandise Mart was for some time owned by Joseph P. Kennedy Sr., who in 1953 commissioned eight bronze busts that would come to be known as the "Merchandise Mart Hall of Fame."

FRANKLIN STREET

Savvy shoppers will recognize their names. Among them are Frank Winfield Woolworth, Aaron Montgomery Ward, John Wanamaker, Edward Albert Filene, and Marshall Field.

The Merchandise Mart is one of Chicago's premier international business locations, welcoming more than 3,000,000 visitors each year. Sixty percent of the building's area is devoted to wholesale showrooms, and the Mart hosts 16 major trade shows and special events each year. Regrettably for the "Second City," the Merchandise Mart's title as the world's largest office building was relinquished in 1941 when the Pentagon in Washington, DC, was completed.

Opened in 1930, this second-largest indoor aquarium in the world (with 5,000,000 gallons of water and 20,000 fish) was a gift to the city from self-made millionaire John G. Shedd, a protégé of retailer Marshall Field. The Shedd Aquarium is also notable for its architecture, designed by the firm of Graham, Anderson, Probst and White in the grand Beaux Arts tradition that was the rage in Chicago following the World's Columbian Exposition held there in 1893.

LORE & LEGEND

Saltwater and fish for the tanks at the Shedd were transported up from Florida in a specially made railway car called the Nautillus.

JOHN G. SHEDD AQUARIUM

Wild Reef
SHEDD AQUARIUM

UBS
Chicago Tribune

Wild Reef
SHEDD AQUARIUM

UBS
Chicago Tribune

Exit Only

Will Call   Will Call

Membership   Membership

Shedd Aquarium has always been at the forefront of innovation in displaying marine life and habitats. In 1971, a massive 90,000-gallon tank reproducing a Caribbean coral reef was opened, followed in 1991 by the "Oceanarium," featuring Pacific white-sided dolphins and belugas. In 2003 the "Wild Reef" (a re-creation of a Philippine coral reef) was added. Visitors are drawn to a 400,000-gallon shark tank, which features curved, 12-foot-high windows that enable a view of the sharks swimming around them.

This needlelike structure rising above East Wacker Drive was built in 1928, designed in response to a pioneering city ordinance requiring that skyscrapers have "setbacks" as they rose higher, allowing more light and air to reach street level. Rising more than 500 feet, Mather Tower demonstrates that a concentration of soaring edifices need not create dark canyons below. The building's octagonal turret, which is about half the height of the building, gives tenants at the top less than 300 square feet of total floor space.

LORE & LEGEND

Although he never attained the fame of George Pullman, Alonzo Clark Mather (1848–1941) also made his fortune from improving the amenities of rail travel, though not for humans. Mather developed a stock car in which food and

water could be provided to livestock while en route, thus keeping them healthy and reducing their suffering. This invention garnered Mather a medal from the American Humane Society.

Mather Tower combines a modernist form with lush historic ornamentation. In 1998, pieces of its terra-cotta cladding fell from the upper tower, which was surrounded in mesh as a precaution. In 2000, the cupola was declared structurally unsound and removed. However, a declaration of landmark status inspired a complete renovation, and the turret was restored using helicopters to hoist structural pieces from a barge on the Chicago River below.

The first United Methodist Church, founded by Methodist circuit riders in 1831, is the oldest church in Chicago. Over the years, its congregation has worshipped in five different buildings located at the same site at the corner of Washington and Clark Streets. The first building, a wooden structure built in 1834, was replaced by larger buildings in 1845 and 1858, the latter reduced to ashes in the Great Chicago Fire of 1871.

The present skyscraper housing the church, the Chicago Temple Building, was dedicated in 1924, a year after the photo on the facing page was taken. At 568 feet, it was then the tallest building in Chicago. The first-floor sanctuary can seat 1,000 worshippers, and many visitors make a pilgrimage to the Sky Chapel, located under the spire 400 feet over the streets of the city.

The growth of Chicago went hand in hand with improved public transportation. Horse-drawn carriages were replaced by cable cars in 1882. These in turn yielded to electric trolleys in 1906, the year this photo was taken at the corner of West Madison and Franklin (although horses for cartage where still employed).

The entire city block seen in the photo on the opposite page has been replaced by a 40-story skyscraper with the address 1 South Wacker Drive. Designed by Murphy/Jahn Architects and completed in 1982, its incorporation of several deep setbacks lets light filter down to street level, while its reflecting glass sheathing and interesting angles give it the appearance of a soaring pile of glass reflecting the surrounding sky and skyline.

Chicago's Loop is where the train lines serving outer neighborhoods come together to circle the central business district on "L" (elevated railway) tracks. Most assume this configuration gave rise to the term "Loop," while others maintain it derives from the centrally located pulleys that powered earlier cable cars. Actually forming a rectangle (above Lake, Wabash, Van Buren, and Wells Streets), the Loop line is the nerve center of Chicago's rapid transit network and gives its name to the city center. The number of passengers entering and leaving the Loop peaked in 1948 at almost a million per day in each direction.

T he city did not build its first elevated train line until 1892, when the Chicago & South Side Rapid Transit Company used steam locomotives to haul passengers from Congress to 39th Street. Other lines followed suit, and in 1897, streetcar magnate Charles T. Yerkes Jr., who owned the Lake Street "L," completed the Union Elevated Railroad, a downtown loop connecting all four lines. The existing "L"s abandoned their individual downtown terminals and circled the loop, and by 1898 all elevated lines had converted from steam locomotives to electric power.

CLARENCE DARROW

In 1887, the young lawyer moved to Chicago, where he gained fame defending controversial figures. Perhaps Darrow's most famous case was the so-called Monkey Trial, in which he defended teacher John T. Scopes, accused of teaching the evolutionary origins of mankind rather than divine creation.

BENNY GOODMAN

The legendary Chicago-born (1909) clarinetist and bandleader was a high school dropout raised on Maxwell Street. He cut his first record in 1926 and went on to become the ambassador of swing, generally credited for making jazz respectable.

JANE ADDAMS

The founder in 1889 of Chicago's Hull House, which provided neighborhood services such as daycare facilities and an employment bureau, Addams was active in many social and political causes of her day, and in 1931 became the first American woman to receive the Nobel Peace Prize.

AL CAPONE

Chicago's most notorious gangster was actually born in New York. Although he quit school in the sixth grade, he was an "alumnus" of Brooklyn's Rippers and the Forty Thieves Juniors gangs before launching a lucrative career in the saloons and brothels of Chicago.

CYRUS MCCORMICK

The inventor of the grain reaper moved to Chicago in 1847 to serve the vast prairie grain fields of the Midwest. In 1851, his invention won the highest award of the day, the Gold Medal at London's Crystal Palace Exhibition, and Cyrus McCormick became both a world celebrity and a wealthy man.

ANN LANDERS

Esther Pauline Friedman Lederer, a.k.a. Ann Landers, wrote the famous syndicated advice column under that name, a regular feature in many newspapers for some 45 years. Lederer's home for many years was Chicago, where she died in 2002.

JEAN BAPTISTE POINT DU SABLE

An African American from what is now Haiti, he was the pioneer settler of Chicago, building in 1779 the first permanent structure on the north bank of the Chicago River just east of the present Michigan Avenue Bridge.

WALT DISNEY

The creator of Mickey Mouse, producer of the first full-length animated movie, inventor the theme park, and architect of the modern multimedia corporation was born in Chicago in 1901.

FRANK LLOYD WRIGHT

In the Chicago suburb of Oak Park can be found the world's largest collection of buildings and houses designed by Frank Lloyd Wright, with 25 structures built between 1889 and 1913. There, the master architect developed and perfected his signature Prairie Style architecture, emphasizing low, horizontal buildings with open spaces.

FAMOUS CHICAGOANS { NOW }

OPRAH WINFREY

Oprah came to Chicago in 1984 to host WLS-TV's *AM Chicago*, later renamed *The Oprah Winfrey Show*. The program became the number one talk show in national syndication in less than a year, eventually making Oprah not only one of *Time* magazine's "100 Most Influential People of the 20th Century," but also the first female African-American billionaire.

HARRISON FORD

Born in Chicago in 1942, he was a lackluster student at Maine Township High School in suburban Park Ridge and later a college dropout before heading for Hollywood to become the hero or heartthrob of nearly every man and woman on the planet.

PAT SAJAK

The host of television's *Wheel of Fortune* game show since 1981 was born in Chicago in 1946 and grew up there as well. He attended Columbia College while working nights as a desk clerk at the Palmer House Hotel.

MICHAEL JORDAN

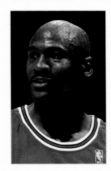

Although born in Brooklyn, Michael Jordan's name is synonymous with the world-champion Chicago Bulls basketball team, which he led to six NBA championships during the 1990s. The top player of his era, Jordan is widely thought to be the best player ever to wear an NBA uniform.

QUINCY JONES

Born on Chicago's South Side in 1933, Quincy Delight Jones Jr. is the most nominated Grammy artist of all time, with a total of 76 nominations and 26 awards (not to mention his Emmy Award and seven Oscar nominations).

DOROTHY HAMILL

The Chicago native won the gold medal in women's ice skating at the 1976 Olympics in Innsbruck, Austria, and became the most sought-after figure skater for commercial endorsements in history. She starred in the Ice Capades for many years and was inducted into the U.S. Figure Skating Hall of Fame in 1991.

JOHN CUSACK AND JOAN CUSACK

Popular actor John Cusack was born in the Chicago suburb of Evanston in 1966 and still resides in Chicago. His actress sister Joan is an alum of *Saturday Night Live* and provided the voice for Jessica the yodeling cowgirl in *Toy Story 2*.

HILLARY RODHAM CLINTON

Born in Chicago in 1947, Hilary Rodham graduated from Yale Law School, where she met her husband, future president Bill Clinton. She is the first former First Lady ever elected to the U.S. Senate, representing the state of New York.

GENE SISKEL AND ROGER EBERT

Gene Siskel, film critic of the *Chicago Tribune* along with Roger Ebert, film critic of the *Chicago Sun-Times*, hosted the first and most popular of the movie review programs that emerged on television in the 1970s. (Gene Siskel died in 1999, and his role is now filled by Richard Roeper.)

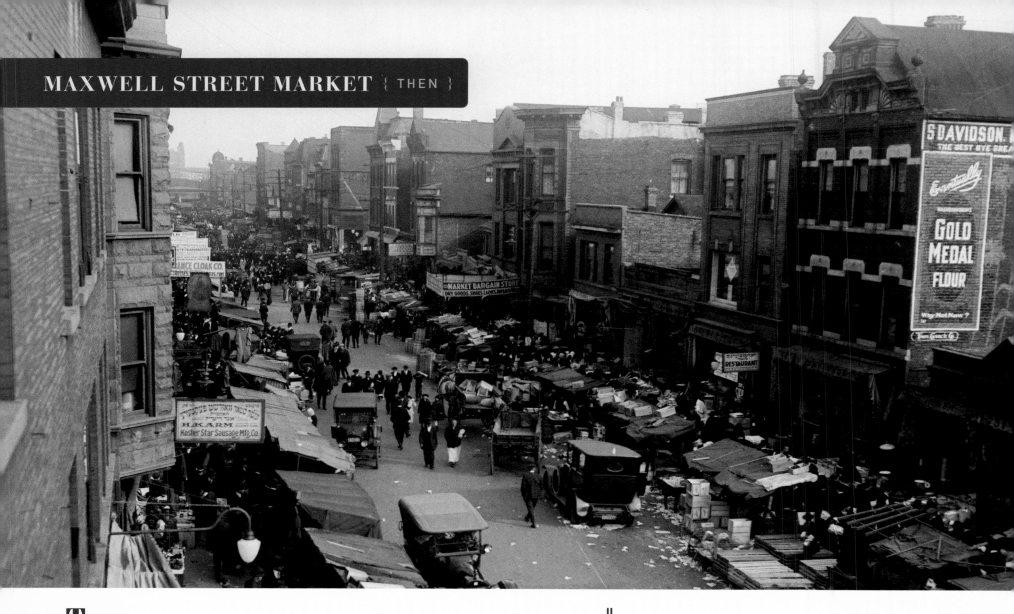

The Near West Side of Chicago has traditionally been a vibrant and colorful area, home to working-class immigrants from many countries. Merchants with pushcarts serviced the needs of the community with low-cost goods, and the Maxwell Street Market was formally established in 1912. Regarded by many as the true soul of Chicago, Maxwell Street of yesteryear was a place where people from all races and backgrounds felt comfortable mixing, enjoying ethnic food, listening to free blues music, and finding great bargains.

Unfortunately, Maxwell Street has not fared well at the hands of urban renewal. One of the last undeveloped sites in an area becoming increasingly gentrified, the market was "moved" in 1994 to a spot on Canal Street and Roosevelt Road, about a half-mile east of the old location. Although old-timers say it lacks the full flavor of the original, this New Maxwell Street Market is certainly worth a visit and remains a great spot for shopping and people watching.

In the late ninteenth century, an organized labor movement was underway to reduce the working day to eight hours. Responding to strikes called for May 1, 1886, 35,000 workers walked off their jobs. During a peaceful rally on May 4 at Haymarket Square, someone threw a bomb, killing one policeman instantly; eight more died later, and hundreds of workers were killed or wounded. Eight prominent anarchists were tried for the crime, despite a lack of evidence. Four were hung and one committed suicide; the three others were later pardoned.

The events at Haymarket Square inspired the establishment of May Day as the traditional celebration of the international working class and labor movement (although, it is not an official holiday in the United States). To commemorate the international significance of the Haymarket tragedy, the City of Chicago unveiled a new monument on September 18, 2004, by Chicago artist Mary Brogger; it portrays a 15-foot speakers' wagon at the spot where labor leaders addressed the crowd in 1886.

J ust 28 years old when he moved to Chicago in 1859, industrialist George Pullman made a fortune with his luxury railroad cars, especially the sleeping cars that bear his name. Before Pullman, rail travel was hot, dusty, and noisy. Pullman's cars featured gourmet dining, comfortable lounges, and sleeper compartments with fine sheets and pillows. In 25 years, Pullman expanded his operations and overcame his competitors until he controlled the industry.

LORE & LEGEND

George Pullman was buried at night, in a pit eight feet deep, with floors and walls of steel-reinforced concrete. Ambrose Bierce remarked, "It is clear the family in their bereavement was making sure the sonofabitch wasn't going to get up and come back." In reality, the family wanted to prevent labor activitists from being able to dig up his body.

Around his railroad car factory, George Pullman created an entire town to house his workers and their families, a project that won him some regard as an enlightened employer. When hard times came, however, he refused to reduce rents to reflect the cuts he had made in wages, and harsh treatment of strikers at his Pullman works in 1894 made clear his antilabor position. He died a bitter man in 1897. But his town survives as the historic Pullman District, today both a National Historic and City of Chicago landmark district.

M ale workers from South China began arriving in the United States in the 1850s, when the wages of even a menial job would both support them and allow them to send money home; thousands were employed building the Transcontinental Railroad. When that was completed, they migrated eastward, first arriving in Chicago in the 1870s and settling near the Loop. After 1910, the workers moved south to an area around Cermak and Wentworth Avenues, where rents were cheaper.

Although now squeezed into an eight-block strip by the construction of major expressways on both sides, Chicago's Chinatown continues to flourish and is home to more than a third of all Chinese in the city. Its more than fifty Asian restaurants, grocery stores, and gift shops are a major tourist attraction, and it remains a welcoming port for new Chinese immigrants, at least at their initial stage of adjustment. Although a "New Chinatown" area has been established along Argyle Street on the North Side, it has attracted more Vietnamese and Koreans than Chinese; in fact, it is usually called "Small Saigon."

In 1894, Judge Lambert Tree established a residence for struggling artists called Tree Studios; he later sold adjacent property to the Shriners service organization. There, in 1913, they completed their new headquarters, the Medinah Temple, a rare and glorious example of Islamic Revival architecture. The Shriners later acquired the whole city block but, by the 1990s, had decided to cash in on their increasingly valuable property by selling to developers, who planned to put up a high-rise tower and parking garage.

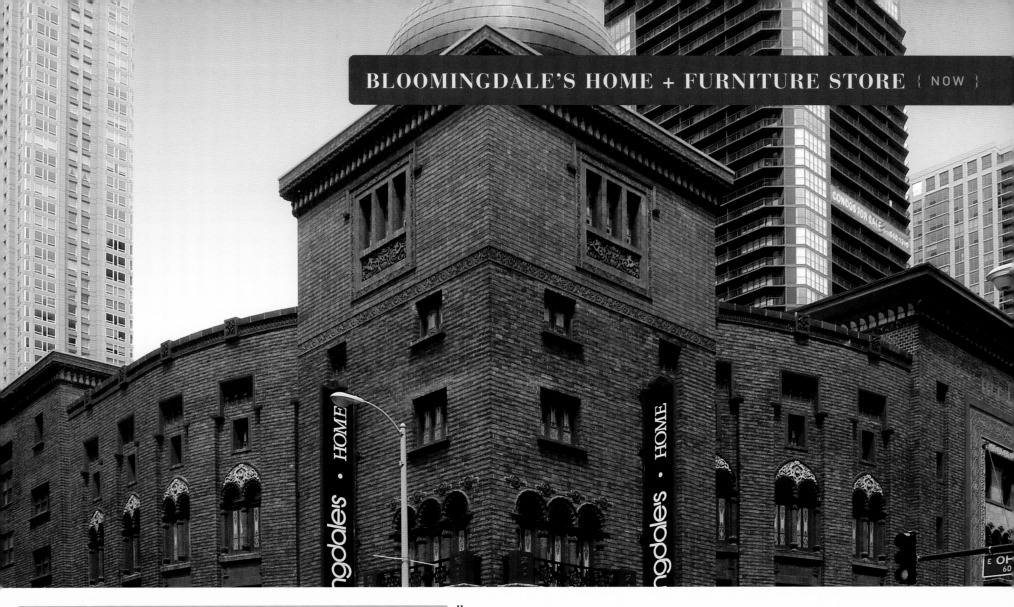

LORE & LEGEND

Joining in the bitter struggle over preservation, the World Monuments Fund named Tree Studios one of the world's 100 most endangered places, right next to Machu Picchu and the Valley of the Kings.

A long and bitter battle over landmark status, which would have limited development, resulted in a compromise. Both Medinah Temple and Tree Studios were declared Chicago Landmarks and have been preserved through a $60-million renovation project. The tranquil rooms and courtyard of the Tree Studios are now open to the public, although artists are no longer in residence. The facade and details of the Medinah Temple are preserved, but its vast auditorium is now a Bloomingdale's Home + Furniture Store.

By the turn of the twentieth century, Chicago had become a national center for the manufacturing of musical instruments, supplying half of all the pianos sold in the country. A marketing competition for the "best piano" at Chicago's Columbian Exposition of 1893 generated nationwide publicity for local brands, including Hamilton (later Baldwin), Story & Clark, Bush & Gerts, and the W. W. Kimball Company, which became the largest single producer of pianos and organs in the world.

LORE & LEGEND

"Coin-pianos" and "orchestrions" were the precursors of the modern jukebox. Chicago manufacturers included the J. P. Seeburg Company, which, along with Wurlitzer, came to dominate post–World War II jukebox production.

Many of the more than 40 companies manufacturing pianos, organs, and other instruments had showrooms on Wabash Avenue, which came to be known as "Music Row." The Bush Temple of Music on West Chicago Avenue was opened by the Bush & Gerts Piano Company as its headquarters and showroom in 1901. Designed by J.E.O. Pridmore, it is considered a rare surviving example of the French Renaissance Revival style not only in Chicago but also in the entire country. In 2001, a century after its completion, it was designated a Chicago Landmark.

Across Michigan Avenue in Grant Park, two stone lions guard the entrance to The Art Institute of Chicago. The origins of this museum and school date to 1866, when local artists established the Chicago Academy of Design in rented rooms on Clark Street. The present classical Beaux Arts building dates from 1893, the year of the World's Columbian Exposition, which was held in Chicago. The institute has expanded considerably since then, building eastward over the tracks of the Illinois Central Railroad that run behind it, and now houses one of the world's greatest collections of artistic treasures.

O ver the years, the institute's goals as a school—a place offering cutting-edge training in all styles and media—and as a museum—a conservator of the finest works from present and past—have sometimes clashed. However, most would agree that the result is not only an internationally renowned museum holding a premier collection of art from around the globe, but also an art school ranked as one of the best in the country. The institute's Ryerson and Burnham Libraries are also considered premier research facilities for the study of art and architecture.

The "CBOT" was established in 1848 by 82 merchants seeking a dependable, centralized marketplace for the purchase and sale of agricultural commodities. Today it is the world's oldest options and futures exchange, with worldwide members trading contracts for everything from silver and gold to wheat and soybeans to ethanol and interest rates. Due to huge growth in trading, the CBOT constructed a building at LaSalle Street and Jackson Boulevard in 1885; it was the city's tallest building at the time.

LORE & LEGEND

The Board of Trade's first building was destroyed by the Great Fire of 1871. The exchange closed for two weeks, then reopened in a temporary 90-by-90-foot wigwam at Washington and Market Streets.

LORE & LEGEND

The statue of Ceres on the Board of Trade Building is faceless because its sculptor believed that no one could possibly see it mounted atop a 45-story building.

In 1930 CBOT moved into its new 45-story home at the LaSalle and Jackson location. Holabird & Root designed the 605-foot, Art Deco building, the city's first commercial structure that had electrical lighting. Topped by a 30-foot statue of Ceres, the Greek goddess of grain, the CBOT building was designated a Chicago Landmark in 1977. In 2006, CBOT merged with Chicago Merchantile Exchange Holdings, Inc., creating the most extensive gloal derivatives exchange.

Barney and Abe Balaban entered the business of showing "moving pictures" in 1908 by leasing the Kedzie Nickelodeon, which had seating for 100. Dreaming of a huge chain of grand movie houses, they partnered with Sam and Morris Katz in 1916. The resulting Balaban and Katz Theater Corporation perfected the concept of "movie palaces" as huge, sumptuously appointed auditoriums where audiences could watch both movies and live performances in comfort and luxury. The Chicago Theatre was the first such building in America and the prototype for all others.

LORE & LEGEND

When the theatre opened in 1921, a staff of 125 ushers escorted guests to their seats. Patrons paid 25 cents until 1 PM, 35 cents in the afternoon, and 50 cents after 6 PM.

Designed by Cornelius and George Rapp in the Beaux Arts style and completed in 1921, the exterior features a miniature replica of the Arc de Triomphe above the six-story State Street marquee. The five-story lobby is modeled after the Royal Chapel at Versailles, and the grand staircase—modeled on that of the Paris Opera House—leads patrons to the 3,600-seat auditorium soaring seven stories. Although few of the hundreds of movie palaces built by Balaban and Katz survive, Chicago boasts three, including the landmarked Uptown and Chicago theaters.

What's all this about Chicago being the "Second City"?

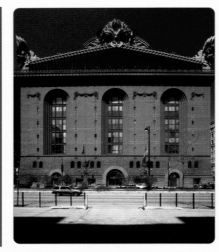

Chicago's **HAROLD WASHINGTON LIBRARY** is the world's largest public library.

THE ADLER PLANETARIUM was the first planetarium in the western hemisphere.

THE ART INSTITUTE OF CHICAGO holds the largest collection of Impressionist paintings in the western hemisphere (actually, in the world outside of the Louvre in Paris).

THE JOHN G. SHEDD AQUARIUM is the largest indoor aquarium in the world and contains one of the largest and most diverse shark habitats in North America.

CHICAGO BOASTS THREE OF THE WORLD'S TEN TALLEST BUILDINGS, INCLUDING

THE SEARS TOWER at 1,450 feet;

THE JOHN HANCOCK BUILDING at 1,127 feet; and THE AMOCO BUILDING (pictured above, now the Aon Center) at 1,136 feet.

The 2.2 million square feet of Chicago's MCCORMICK PLACE give it the largest amount of exhibit space of any convention center in the country.

AND...

Chicago's NABISCO PLANT at 7300 South Kedzie Avenue is the world's largest cookie and cracker factory.

THE CHICAGO POST OFFICE at 433 West Van Buren Street is the only postal facility in the world that you can drive a car through.

Chicago's KEEBLER PLANT at 10839 South Langley Avenue is the world's largest ice cream cone factory.

Chicago's MEXICAN FINE ARTS CENTER MUSEUM is the largest Latino cultural institution in the nation.

Who needs the coasts, anyway? Chicago's 30 miles of lakefront include 15 miles of BATHING BEACHES.

FIELD MUSEUM, JACKSON PARK { THEN }

A natural history museum for Chicago had been planned for some time prior to the World's Columbian Exposition in 1893. The close of that event left the Palace of Fine Arts Building in Jackson Park vacant; it reopened in 1894 as the Field Museum of Natural History, with the support of a million-dollar donation from retail magnate Marshall Field. Originally housing the biological and anthropological collections assembled for the exposition, new acquisitions soon overwhelmed the capacity of the existing structure, and a new building was planned.

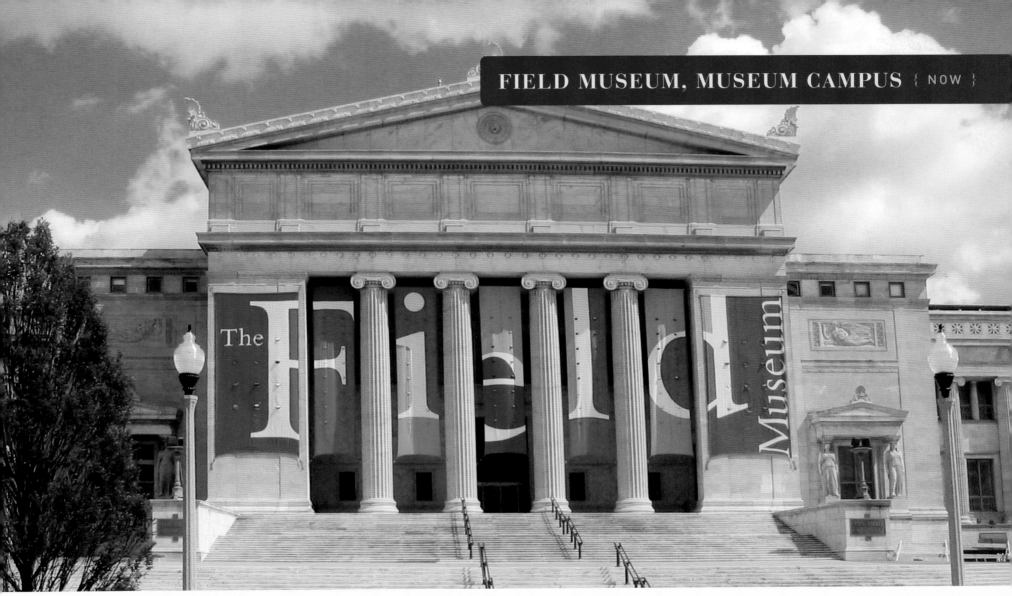

A new white marble building, reminiscent of the former building but vaster in scale, opened to the public in 1921 on the "Museum Campus" of Grant Park, joining the John G. Shedd Aquarium and the Adler Planetarium. The building was funded by Marshall Field's nephew, Stanley, who donated $2 million and served as the museum's president for 56 years. Housing more than 20 million specimens and a natural history library of more than 250,000 volumes, the Field Museum is today one of the great natural history museums of the world.

When Chicago's original lakefront City Cemetery was decreed a health hazard due to overcrowding and the possibility of spreading waterborne diseases, the bodies interred there were moved to private cemeteries, including Graceland, established in 1860 on 120 then-quiet suburban acres. (The old City Cemetery became what is now Lincoln Park.) At Graceland, massive oaks and maples stand silently over the tombs and monuments of Chicago's movers and shakers of the past 150 years.

WM. H. MITCHELL

The many architecturally significant tombs and monuments of Graceland bear the great names closely associated with the history of Chicago: retail magnates Marshall Field and Potter Palmer; industrialists George Pullman and Cyrus McCormick; civic planners Daniel Burnham and Charles Wacker; lumber merchant Martin Ryerson; meatpacker Phillip D. Amour; and finally, many world-famous Chicago architects, including John Root, William Holabird, Louis Sullivan, David Adler, and Ludwig Mies van der Rohe.

Orthodox Christians follow the ways of the ancient Byzantine church, and their parishes typically reflect their ethnic identities and heritages. Greeks, Russians, and Serbs were the first Eastern Orthodox believers to establish churches in Chicago. The Greek Orthodox parish of St. Constantine, built in 1909 on the city's South Side, became one of the largest Greek Orthodox congregations in the western hemisphere. The city's Russian immigrants created St. Vladimir's Russian Orthodox parish in 1892 and built Holy Trinity Orthodox Cathedral in 1903.

HOLY TRINITY ORTHODOX CATHEDRAL { NOW }

Resembling the countryside churches that its congregation would fondly recall, the cathedral was in fact designed by noted Chicago School architect Louis Sullivan. It is considered one of his finest minor works, with stucco-covered brick supporting an undulating roofline that is repeated in the rectory inside. A donation of $4,000 from Czar Nicholas II himself supported its construction. By the 1970s, Chicago and its neighborhoods were home to 88 Eastern Orthodox parishes of various ethnic classifications. The Holy Trinty Orthodox Cathedral was designated a Chicago Landmark in 1979.

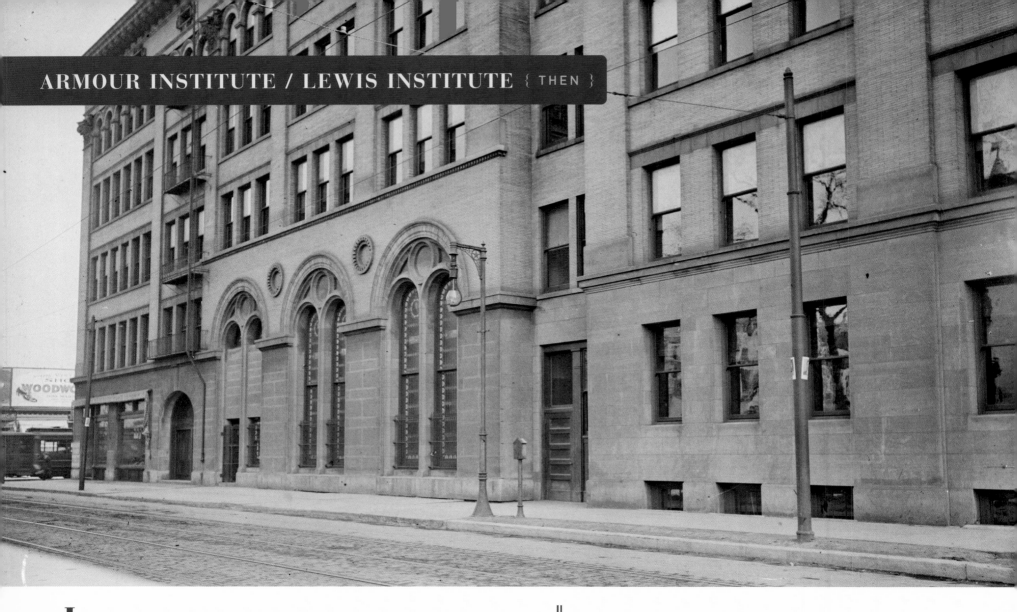

In the nineteenth century, advanced education was generally available only to the elite. Among those supportive of more widespread educational opportunity was wealthy meatpacker Philip Danforth Armour, who agreed to finance a school where students of all backgrounds could prepare for work in a changing industrial society. The Armour Institute opened in 1893. Established two years later, the Lewis Institute (above), offered liberal arts as well as science and engineering courses. The Illinois Institute of Technology was created by the merger of these two schools in 1940.

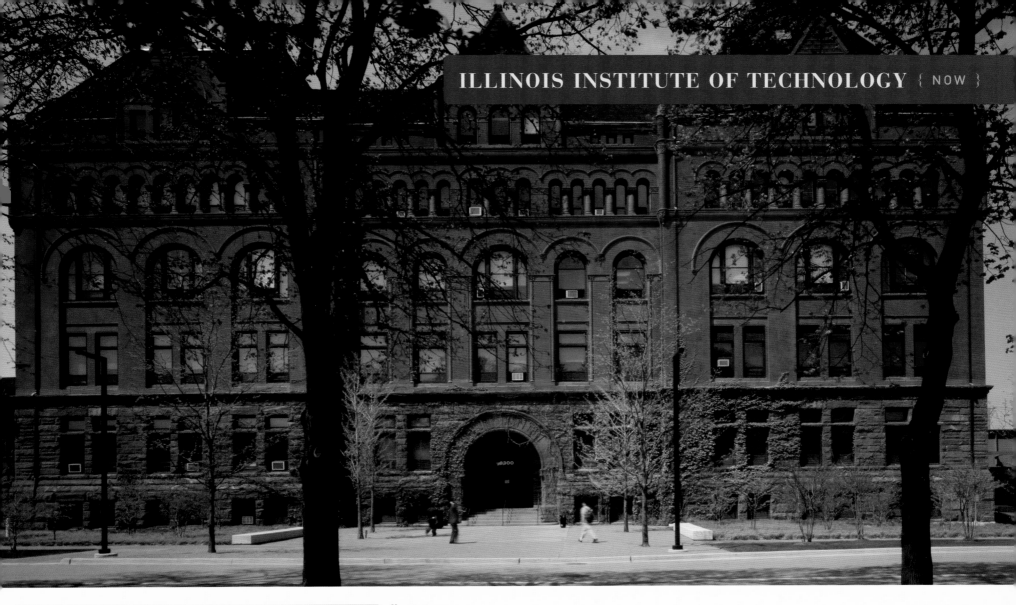

LORE & LEGEND

Many of those unfamiliar with the work of Ludwig Mies van der Rohe (1886–1969) have nonetheless heard his pronouncements on architecture that "less is more" and "God is in the details."

The Illinois Institute of Technology is today a private university with programs in science, engineering, psychology, architecture, business, design, and law. Ludwig Mies van der Rohe, one of the century's most influential architects, headed its architecture program from 1938 to 1958. IIT's 120-acre main campus (including Crown Hall, above, housing the architecture department) was designed by van der Rohe and is recognized by the American Institute of Architects as one of the 200 most significant works of architecture in the United States. IIT-graduated architects have shaped the skylines of cities throughout the world.

Inventor and businessman Cyrus McCormick (1809–1884) moved his reaper factory from Virginia to Chicago in 1847 to take better advantage of his market—the grain-filled prairies of the Midwest. As a result, he amassed a mighty fortune and left his name permanently associated with his new city. His descendants would occupy homes along Lake Shore Drive—Chicago's "Gold Coast"—and country estates in the wealthiest northern suburbs. McCormicks became important figures in banking, investment, news media, and real estate.

LORE & LEGEND

"The Colonel" Robert R. McCormick often ran "hatchet job" stories on his enemies in his *Chicago Tribune*. One headline described the 1936 Democratic Convention as "Soviets Gather in Philadelphia."

The family name today is perhaps familiar to most through McCormick Place, the exhibition space named after descendent Robert R. McCormick (1880–1955). The ultraconservative president of the *Chicago Tribune* recognized Chicago's need for such a facility and led the effort to ensure its construction. Although he did not live to see his dream realized, the first McCormick Place opened its doors in 1960, only to be destroyed by fire in 1967. A new facility opened in 1971 and has steadily grown to become the nation's largest convention center today.

Chicago Municipal Airport, the city's first, opened in 1927 and was renamed Chicago Midway Airport in 1949 to honor those who fought in the decisive Battle of Midway of World War II. In the early postwar years, Midway was the world's busiest air terminal, but it lost that title after 1958 as traffic moved to O'Hare; for the next two decades, Midway was virtually a local airfield. However, O'Hare alone was unable to keep up with exploding air traffic, and today Midway is again a partner in providing Chicago's aviation transportation needs.

LORE & LEGEND

Although located in the heart of the Midwest, O'Hare ranks fourth in the nation in number of international connections; only JFK in New York City, Los Angeles, and Miami international airports serve more foreign destinations.

Located 17 miles northwest of the Chicago Loop, Orchard Field was built as a manufacturing plant for Douglas airplanes during World War II; it was renamed in 1949 after Edward "Butch" O'Hare, a World War II flying ace who was awarded the Medal of Honor. By the early 1950s, the city began to develop O'Hare to replace the overcrowded Midway, and the arrival of Midway's former traffic instantly made O'Hare the new World's Busiest Airport. Today, O'Hare battles annually for that title with the Hartsfield-Jackson Atlanta International Airport.

Despite widespread agreement that the lakefront should remain a public space, defending that goal has required constant effort. By 1847 an area of lakefront property was set aside for "Lake Park," but it remained a mix of squatters' homes and garbage dumps. After the Great Fire of 1871, the area between the Illinois Central railroad tracks and Lake Michigan was used as a landfill for the debris from the city's ruins. As a result, the Illinois Central train tracks were now in the center of the park, creating an eyesore that would not be completely removed for more than a century.

The newest jewel in the crown of Grant Park is the 24-acre Millennium Park, completed in 2004. This combined park, garden, underground parking garage, and cultural center covers the unsightly former rail yard and parking lot of the Illinois Central Railroad. In keeping with Chicago's penchant for great public works, it includes contributions from some of the world's great artists and architects: a music pavilion and bridge by Frank Gehry; a dance theater by Thomas Beeby; a fountain by Jaume Plensa; and a sculpture (above) created by Anish Kapoor.

Experience selling in rural areas gave Aaron Montgomery Ward the revolutionary idea of servicing that market directly. In 1872, he established the world's first mail-order business. The business was so successful that by 1890 he had commissioned and moved into a splendid new tower, then the tallest building in the city. Ward also fought to beautify Chicago's lakefront, opposing developers and city planners for years in the courts. Through his efforts, the area was preserved as the magnificent public space of Grant Park.

LORE & LEGEND

In 1946, the Montgomery Ward Catalog was selected by the Grolier Club, an organization of bibliophiles, to be featured in its exhibition of the 100 American books most influential on the life and culture of the nation.

Montgomery Ward's slogan, "satisfaction guaranteed or your money back," was a winner. Although the first catalog was only 32 pages long, in less than 25 years it grew to 1,000 pages and generated annual sales of $7 million. Completed in 1908, the company's 1.25-million-square-foot center for mail-order shipping, is a dramatic 600-foot-long geometric shape hugging the North Branch of the Chicago River. One of the finest examples of a Chicago School–style industrial building, it is both a Chicago Landmark and a National Historic Landmark.

Charles A. Comiskey wanted to build a home for his White Sox baseball team on 15 acres he had purchased on the South Side of Chicago. Architect Zachary Taylor Davis designed the modern steel-and-glass stadium with sloping Romanesque archways and red-pressed brick that blended in with the ethnic churches of the neighborhood. Ground was broken for the "baseball palace of the world" in early 1910, and the White Sox played their first game there the same year. Here, fans line up for tickets on opening day of the 1914 season.

LORE & LEGEND

The tradition of playing the "Star-Spangled Banner" at baseball games started at Comiskey Park during the World Series of 1918, when American soldiers were fighting in France.

O ver the next 80 years, nearly 73 million fans paid to see games at Comiskey. By 1990, however, this oldest professional baseball park in operation needed to be replaced, and a new stadium was built directly adjacent. In September of 1990, the White Sox played their last game at old Comiskey; they played their first game at the new park the following spring, but not until the infield dirt was moved from the old park to the new. Still home to the White Sox, the stadium was renamed in 2003 to reflect its new corporate sponsorship.

Sports in Chicago

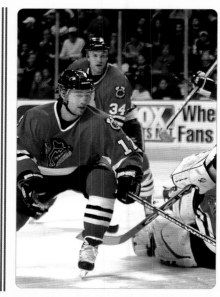

Long-time viewers of *Saturday Night Live* will recall the hilarious series of sketches in which "Superfans" of Chicago's Bears and Bulls discussed the exploits of their teams with passion and metaphysical depth while loading up on beer and brats in their favorite sports bar. To the question, "What is God's role in this?" the answer was that God was obviously a Bears fan: "Otherwise, he wouldn't have put 'em in Chicago."

This pronouncement makes perfect sense to anyone familiar with Chicago's regard for "Da Bears," its beloved National Football League team. They have given the city eight league championships and a Super Bowl victory.

The Bears are just one of 16 professional sports teams in a great city of sports fans, and one of the very few to support two baseball teams, the Cubs of the National League, who play at Wrigley Field, and the White Socks, whose home stadium is U.S.Cellular Field (formerly New Comiskey Park).

The Chicago Bulls of the National Basketball Association are perhaps the most recognized basketball team in the world, chiefly due to the exploits of Michael Jordan, who led his team to six national championships. In one *SNL* sketch, speculation centered on how many points Michael Jordan might score if he played the entire game himself while sitting in a recliner.

The Chicago Blackhawks of the National Hockey League, the Chicago Fire of Major League Soccer, and the Chicago Sky of the Women's NBA all enjoy the support of Chicago's loyal and enthusiastic sports fans.

In 1966, **BOBBY HULL** made more than 50 goals in the '65–'66 season and set an National Hockey League record.

One of the greatest running backs of all time, **WALTER PAYTON** rushed for 16,726 yards with 100 touchdowns for the Bears from 1975 through 1987.

Chicago is one of three U.S. cities officially bidding to host the 2016 **SUMMER OLYMPICS** and is considered a strong contender.

MICHAEL JORDAN was the NBA's Most Valuable Player in three seasons and holds the record for most points, 63, in a single playoff game..

THE BEARS

The global Special Olympics movement got its start in 1968, when the first international **SPECIAL OLYMPICS GAMES** were held at Soldier Field.

B efore the "Gold Coast" along North Lakeshore Drive became the city's most prestigious residential address, the wealthy built their stately mansions along Prairie Avenue, a north–south boulevard that ran from 16th Street southward near the lakefront. Prairie Avenue was close to the Loop, and its residents did not have to cross the Chicago River to do business in the city. Daniel Thompson built the first large home there in 1870, followed by Marshall Field in 1871, and George Pullman (whose house is pictured here) in 1873.

Prairie Avenue was declared a historic district in 1978, though only a few mansions remain there today. A museum for the district has been established in the home designed by Boston-based architect Henry Hobson Richardson and completed in 1887 for International Harvester Company executive John J. Glessner. With its fortresslike Romanesque Revival facade protecting an interior courtyard and rooms from the noise and dirt of an encroaching city, the design presaged the end of Prairie Avenue as a desirable neighborhood. The Glessner House was designated a Chicago Landmark in 1970.

A great city needed a great library, and in 1872, a library board was established and charged to make books available to the "common man." During its first 24 years, the library lacked a permanent home, until a new facility opened at 78 East Washington Street in 1897. Both the architecture and the books inside the grand Classical Revival–style building were intended to uplift and inspire; the interior was decorated with mosaics, marbles, bronze, and stained-glass domes. The building was designated a Chicago Landmark in 1976.

LORE & LEGEND

The first home of the city's library was actually a circular water tank that had survived the Great Fire of 1871.

Extensive renovations over the years could not avert the eventual need for a larger and more technologically modern space. A "design and build" competition was held and funded with a bond issue of $144 million. In 1991, the largest public library building in the world, the Harold Washington Library Center—named after the late mayor who had spearheaded the project—opened to the public on South State Street. The former Chicago Public Library became the Chicago Cultural Center and is home to various arts programs and the city's cultural affairs department.

Built between 1925 and 1928 (when this photograph was taken), the chapel was designed in a Byzantine-Romanesque variation of Gothic style by Bertram Goodhue. Named for the famed industrialist, philanthropist, and founder of the University of Chicago—John D. Rockefeller—the chapel is located on the south end of the campus. Rockefeller donated more than $35 million to the university over the course of two decades. In 1910, his final gift came with the stipulation that $1.5 million be used to build a "University Chapel," as it was first called.

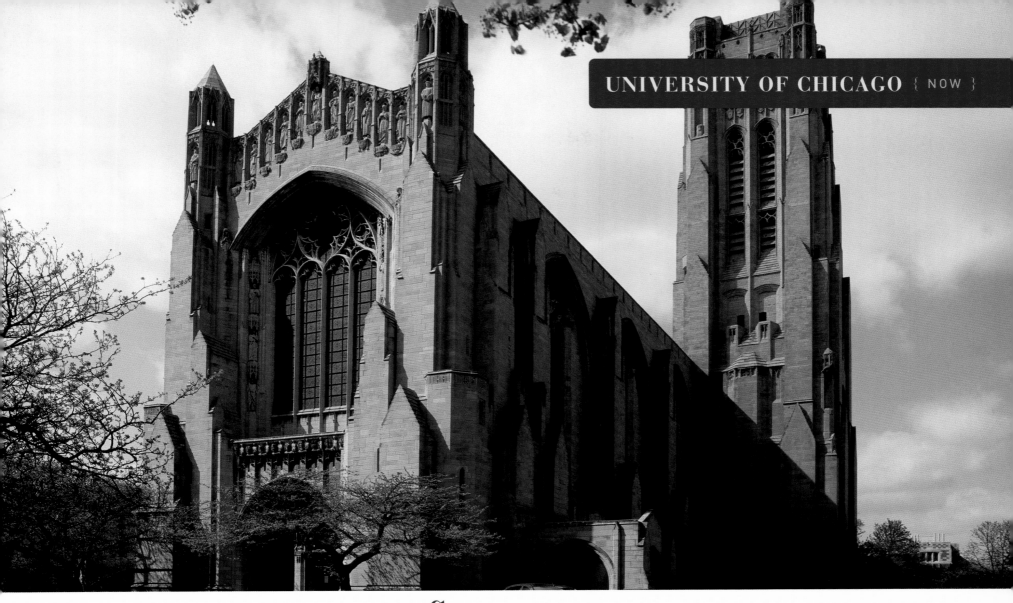

Since its incorporation in 1890, the University of Chicago has grown into one of the greatest educational institutions in the world, with an endowment of more than $4 billion and a campus comprising 136 buildings on 211 acres of the South Side. Over the years, 79 Nobel Prize winners have been associated with the university, either as faculty members, students, or researchers. Rockefeller himself declared the university "the best investment I ever made."

In 1911, the chairman of Sears, Roebuck and Co., Julius Rosenwald, took his son to visit the Deutsches Museum in Munich, which specialized in industrial and scientific processes, and encouraged visitor participation in exhibits. Rosenwald became convinced that Chicago needed such a museum and led the effort to establish one in the former Palace of Fine Arts Building in Jackson Park. This last surviving great structure from the World's Columbian Exposition of 1893 required extensive renovation, which began in 1929 (the year this photograph was taken).

The museum opened concurrently with Chicago's "Century of Progress" World's Fair of 1933. Today it is one of the most popular museums in the country, with approximately 2,000,000 visitors annually wandering its 350,000 square feet (approximately eight acres) and interacting (not just viewing static displays) with more than 2,000 exhibits. Featured attractions include a working replica of a 1933 coal mine elevator, a captured U-505 German submarine, a Boeing 727 that visitors can walk through, and a 3,500-square-foot model railroad, one of the largest in the world.

As a transit point for agricultural products from the West and Midwest that were to be packaged and shipped to the East, Chicago was an important center for meatpacking. The incorporation in 1865 of several smaller stockyards into the 475-acre Union Stock Yard encouraged Philip Armour to build a large pork plant nearby and eventually Chicago's largest meatpacking company. A philanthropist interested in training young people, Armour later established the Armour Institute in 1893, a vocational school that became the Illinois Institute of Technology.

Meatpacker Gustavus F. Swift also saw the merits of a Chicago location and established his headquarters there. By the time of Swift's death in 1903, Swift & Co. employed more than 5,000 workers at its Stock Yard slaughtering plant. By the 1950s, however, interstate trucking and decentralization of the industry brought about its decline. After handling more than one billion animals, the Union Stock Yard closed in 1971. Although the old gate remains, the stockyard site is today home to an industrial park.

Chicago's famed lakefront playing field opened in 1924 as Municipal Grant Park Stadium, though its name was changed to Soldier Field in 1925 as a memorial to fallen American soldiers. The original design was modeled on the Greco-Roman architectural tradition, featuring Doric columns rising above the stands. Many great sporting contests and public events have been held here over the years.

LORE & LEGEND

Unfortunately, New Soldier Field, as its fans came to call it, did not impress the advisory board of the National Register of Historic Places, which removed its landmark designation in 2006, primarily due to the extensive renovations.

When the Chicago Park District, which owns the property, announced its intention to rebuild the home of the Chicago Bears in 2001, the plans were severely criticized. But when the renovation was completed in 2003, it was hailed by such notable architecture critics as Herbert Muschamp of the *New York Times* as one of the five best new buildings of the year. The modern stands now dwarf the original Greek columns, even though the seating capacity (61,500) is smaller than the previous stadium.

CHICAGO STOCK EXCHANGE { THEN }

STEWART WARNER
NAT. CARBON PFD.
UNITED PAPER BD.

CARBIDE
ORPHEUM
INLAND STEEL
WOLFF MNFG.

YELLOW CAB
PINES W.F.

The third most active stock exchange in the United States by volume—and the largest outside of New York City—opened for trading in 1882 in a leased building at 115 Dearborn Street (shown above). As it grew, the CHX moved several times, most notably in 1893 to a new Louis Sullivan–designed building at 30 North LaSalle Street. Although this fine building was demolished in 1972, its trading room is preserved at the Art Institute of Chicago, while its decorated entryway arch stands in the institute's East Garden.

CHICAGO STOCK EXCHANGE { NOW }

CHICAGO STOCK EXCHANGE

AVAILABLE
372-3224

Completed in 1985, the latest home of the exchange features a decidedly "ungrand" box for the trading floor adjacent to a soaring 39-story skyscraper. Although the exchange changed its name to the Midwest Stock Exchange after merging with other local exchanges in 1949, it changed back to its original name in 1993, reflecting Chicago's position as one of the world's great centers of trade. With nine exchanges in all, it is sometimes called the "Exchange Capital of the World."

Yet another of the great department store names associated with Chicago, Carson Pirie Scott was actually founded in Amboy, Illinois, in 1854 by John T. Pirie and Samuel Carson, two Scotch-Irish immigrants; Robert Scott came on as a partner after the store moved to Chicago at the end of the Civil War. Although no longer an independent chain, the Carson name can still be seen on about 30 stores around the Midwest, but is most strongly linked to the flagship store it has occupied since 1904.

Designated a Chicago Landmark in 1970, the Louis Sullivan–designed store at State and Madison Streets is considered one of the most important structures in early modern architecture, and a classic example of the Chicago School buildings considered important precursors to twentieth-century steel-and-glass skyscrapers. Inseparably merging function and beauty, distinctive, large, three-part windows effectively show off the goods and activities within, while the two lowest stories are enveloped in the ornately decorative cast-iron for which Sullivan was justly famous.

Frank Lloyd Wright was a resident of Oak Park and a member of the Unitarian Universalist congregation there when its place of worship was struck by lightning and burned to the ground in 1905. Asked by the parish to design an affordable replacement on property donated by a member of the church, Wright planned and directed construction of Unity Temple (above), one of his earliest public works and one of the great religious buildings of the twentieth century.

LORE & LEGEND

Wright declared the completion of Unity Temple in 1908 as "my contribution to modern architecture." Indeed, its seminal position at the beginning of modern architecture is widely acknowledged.

To stay within his modest budget of $40,000, Wright used reinforced concrete cast in place to create a bold cubical design that broke the bounds of religious architecture. A seemingly stark edifice hides an interior with unpredictable geometric arrangements and decor reminiscent of Native American art; a sanctuary of stucco with wood trim crowned by art-glass skylights bathes worshippers in natural light. The U.S. Department of the Interior designated Unity Temple a National Historic Landmark in 1971.

William Holabird came to Chicago in 1875 and met fellow architect Martin Roche. Both worked for William Le Baron Jenney, whose designs for steel-framed buildings led to the modern skyscraper. In 1881, Holabird and Roche left to form their own firm. In 1908, they designed the 14-story lakefront home of the exclusive University Club of Chicago, located at the corner of Michigan Avenue and Monroe Street.

One of only three Gothic skyscrapers in the country, the University Club of Chicago demonstrates Holabird & Roche's (later Holabird & Root) design versatility. Although closely connected with the architectural movement known as the "Chicago School," the firm designed many of the city's Neoclassical and Art Deco treasures as well. The University Club of Chicago still operates as an exclusive organization that provides a place where members can meet to discuss business, social, and cultural issues.

Resources for Further Exploration

The Chicago World's Fair of 1893: A Photographic Record.
Applebaum, Stanley.
Mineola, New York: Dover Publications, 1980.
The Columbian Exposition was planned to demonstrate to the world that the city was not only well and thriving after its disastrous fire two decades earlier, but could also entertain all comers in gracious and sophisticated style.

Chicago Days: 150 Defining Moments in the Life of a Great City.
Chicago Tribune.
New York: McGraw-Hill, 1996.
This volume is for those particularly interested in the exciting highlights of the city's history, presented in photographs from the files of the *Chicago Tribune* and the Chicago Historical Society, and in brief essays.

The Encyclopedia of Chicago
Grossman, James R., Ann Durkin Keating, and Janice L. Reiff, eds.
Chicago: University of Chicago Press, 2004.
This is the bible of Chicago history. Ten years in the making, its 1,400 hundred articles in 1,104 pages were authorized by 633 experts and supported with documents, maps, and images from the collections of the Chicago Historical Society, the Newberry Library, and Northwestern University.

Lost Chicago.
Lowe, David Garrad.
New York: Watson-Guptill Publications, 2000.
The focus on architectural treasures now gone, and the many interior and detail shots documenting them make this a special book.

Chicago: Growth of a Metropolis.
Mayer, Harold M., and Richard C. Wade.
Chicago: University of Chicago Press, 1973.
Although containing fewer pages (522) than Professor Miller's books, copious photographs (more than 1,000) and many maps help the reader follow the story. It thoroughly examines the sociological dynamics of the city and its suburbs.

City of the Century: The Epic of Chicago and the Making of America.
Miller, Donald L.
New York: Simon and Schuster, 1997.
For those who want a readable and comprehensive history of the city, Miller, professor of history at Lafayette University, chronicles Chicago's growth and development, and recounts the colorful stories of those who made it happen.

Chicago at the Turn of the Century in Photographs: 122 Historic Views from the Collections of the Chicago Historical Society.
Viskochil, Larry A.
Mineola, New York: Dover Publications, 1984.
The author, curator of prints and photographs at the Chicago Historical Society, presents selected images from a collection of 300 donated to the society in 1938 by the Barnes-Crosby Company, one of Chicago's largest photo engraving firms.

Masterpieces of Chicago Architecture.
Zukowsky, John, and Martha Thorne.
New York: Rizzoli, 2004.
The curator and associate curator of architecture, respectively, at the Art Institute of Chicago this comprehensive review of the city's architectural legacy, using images from the Art Institute's collection of 150,000 drawings, photographs, and models.

Photo Credits

Page 2   Image (DN-0082566) courtesy of the Chicago History Museum
Pages 5–6   © Wernher Krutein/Photovault
Page 6   © Wernher Krutein/Photovault
Page 8   Image (DN-0083803) courtesy of the Chicago History Museum
Page 10   © CORBIS
Page 11   © Maps.com/CORBIS
Page 12   Image (DN-083837B) courtesy of the Chicago History Museum
Page 13   © Wernher Krutein/Photovault
Page 14   Image (DN-0070393) courtesy of the Chicago History Museum
Page 15   © Wernher Krutein/Photovault
Page 16   Image (DN-0062947) courtesy of the Chicago History Museum
Page 17   © Wernher Krutein/Photovault
Page 18   Image (DN-0086931) courtesy of the Chicago History Museum
Page 19   © Wernher Krutein/Photovault
Page 20   Image (DN-0077820) courtesy of the Chicago History Museum
Page 21   © Wernher Krutein/Photovault
Page 22   left © Hulton Archive/Getty Images; right © Retrofile/Getty Images
Page 23   © David Hume Kennerly/Getty Images
Page 24   Image (ICHI-31909) courtesy of the Chicago History Museum
Page 25   © Schenectady Museum; Hall of Electrical History Foundation/CORBIS
Page 26   Image (DN-0066201) courtesy of the Chicago History Museum
Page 27   © Wernher Krutein/Photovault
Page 28   Image (DN-0009987) courtesy of the Chicago History Museum
Page 29   © Andrey Popov/shutterstock.com
Page 30   Image (DN-0089139) courtesy of the Chicago History Museum
Page 31   © Wernher Krutein/Photovault
Page 32   Image (DN-0000945) courtesy of the Chicago History Museum
Page 33   Image courtesy of Skidmore, Owings & Merrill LLP
Page 34   Image (DN-0010137A) courtesy of the Chicago History Museum
Page 35   © Wernher Krutein/Photovault
Page 36   Image (DN-0007701) courtesy of the Chicago History Museum
Page 37   © Wernher Krutein/Photovault
Page 38   Image (SDN-064146) courtesy of the Chicago History Museum
Page 39   © Wernher Krutein/Photovault
Page 41   © Wernher Krutein/Photovault
Page 42   Image (DN-0001447A) courtesy of the Chicago History Museum
Page 43   Wayne Lorentz/www.ChicagoArchitecture.info
Page 44   Image (DN-0052025) courtesy of the Chicago History Museum
Page 45   © Sandy Felsenthal/CORBIS
Page 46   Image (DN-0084840) courtesy of the Chicago History Museum
Page 47   © Wernher Krutein/Photovault
Page 48   Image (DN-0056870) courtesy of the Chicago History Museum
Page 49   © Wernher Krutein/Photovault
Page 50   Image (SDN-010065) courtesy of the Chicago History Museum
Page 51   © Bettmann/CORBIS
Page 52   Image (DN-0003365) courtesy of the Chicago History Museum
Page 53   © Wernher Krutein/Photovault
Page 54   Image (DN-0001231) courtesy of the Chicago History Museum
Page 55   © Wernher Krutein/Photovault
Page 56   Image (DN-0074013) courtesy of the Chicago History Museum
Page 57   Image courtesy of The Drake Hotel

Page 58   Image (DN-0081910) courtesy of the Chicago History Museum
Page 59   © Wernher Krutein/Photovault
Page 60   © David P. Smith/shutterstock.com
Page 61   © Klaus Sailer/shutterstock.com
Page 62   Image (DN-0056251) courtesy of the Chicago History Museum
Page 63   © Wernher Krutein/Photovault
Page 64   Image (DN-0079030) courtesy of the Chicago History Museum
Page 65   © Wernher Krutein/Photovault
Page 66   Image (DN-0090076) courtesy of the Chicago History Museum
Page 67   © Wernher Krutein/Photovault
Page 68   Image (DN-0089821) courtesy of the Chicago History Musuem
Page 69   © Wernher Krutein/Photovault
Page 70   Image (DN-0090221) courtesy of the Chicago History Museum
Page 71   © Wernher Krutein/Photovault
Page 72   Image (DN-0085236) courtesy of the Chicago History Museum
Page 73   © Wernher Krutein/Photovault
Page 74   Image (DN-0075439) courtesy of the Chicago History Museum
Page 75   © Wernher Krutein/Photovault
Page 76   Image (DN-0050842) courtesy of the Chicago History Museum
Page 77   © Wernher Krutein/Photovault
Page 78   Image (DN-0003654A) courtesy of the Chicago History Museum
Page 79   © Wernher Krutein/Photovault
Page 80   left/upper © CORBIS; left/lower © Bettmann/CORBIS; middle/upper © Bettmann/CORBIS; middle/lower © Bettmann/CORBIS; right © Bettmann/CORBIS
Page 81   left © Steve Sands/New York Newswire/CORBIS; middle © Duomo/CORBIS; right © Joe Sohm/Chromosohm/jupiterimages.com
Page 82   © Bettmann/CORBIS
Page 83   © Wernher Krutein/Photovault
Page 84   Image (DN-0057584) courtesy of the Chicago History Museum
Page 85   Photograph by Ward Miller, Chicago, Illinois
Page 86   Image (DN-0001761) courtesy of the Chicago History Museum
Page 87   © Wernher Krutein/Photovault
Page 88   Image (DN-0085838) courtesy of the Chicago History Museum
Page 89   © Wernher Krutein/Photovault
Page 90   Image (DN-0061156) courtesy of the Chicago History Museum
Page 91   © Wernher Krutein/Photovault
Page 92   Image (DN-0003430) courtesy of the Chicago History Museum
Page 93   © Grant Kessler 2007
Page 94   Image (DN-0074944) courtesy of the Chicago History Museum
Page 95   © Wernher Krutein/Photovault
Page 96   Image (DN-0087261) courtesy of the Chicago History Museum
Page 97   © Panoramic Images/Getty Images
Page 98   Image (DN-0082072) courtesy of the Chicago History Museum
Page 99   © Wernher Krutein/Photovault
Page 100   All © Wernher Krutein/Photovault
Page 101   upper/left and right © Wernher Krutein/Photovault; left/lower © Richard Cummins/CORBIS
Page 102   Image (DN-0052479) courtesy of the Chicago History Museum
Page 103   © Leslie Stodden/shutterstock.com
Page 104   Image (DN-0070162) courtesy of the Chicago History Museum

Page 105   © Wernher Krutein/Photovault
Page 106   Image (DN-0002191) courtesy of the Chicago History Museum
Page 107   Photograph by Ward Miller, Chicago, Illinois
Page 108   Image (DN-0055639) courtesy of the Chicago History Museum
Page 109   Courtesy of the Illinois Institute of Technology
Page 110   Image (DN-0076818) courtesy of the Chicago History Museum
Page 111   © Wernher Krutein/Photovault
Page 112   Image (DN-0088750) courtesy of the Chicago History Museum
Page 113   © Wernher Krutein/Photovault
Page 114   Image (DN-0085147) courtesy of the Chicago History Museum
Page 115   © Wernher Krutein/Photovault
Page 116   Image (DN-0001233) courtesy of the Chicago History Museum
Page 117   Photograph by Ward Miller, Chicago, Illinois
Page 118   Image (SDN-060615) courtesy of the Chicago History Museum
Page 119   © Robert Maass/CORBIS
Page 120   upper © Frank Polich/Reuters/CORBIS; lower © Bettmann/CORBIS
Page 121   upper/left © Bettmann/CORBIS; upper/middle © Ian Waldie/Getty Images; upper/right © Reuters/CORBIS; lower/left © John Gress/Icon SMI/CORBIS; lower/middle © Karl Weatherly/Getty Images
Page 122   Image (DN-0057957) courtesy of the Chicago History Museum
Page 123   © Wernher Krutein/Photovault
Page 124   Image (DN-0075185) courtesy of the Chicago History Museum
Page 125   © Wernher Krutein/Photovault
Page 126   Image (DN-0086735) courtesy of the Chicago History Museum
Page 127   © Wernher Krutein/Photovault
Page 128   Image (DN-0089973) courtesy of the Chicago History Museum
Page 129   © Wernher Krutein/Photovault
Page 130   Image (DN-0001520) courtesy of the Chicago History Museum
Page 131   Photograph by Ward Miller, Chicago, Illinois
Page 132   Image (DN-0077234) courtesy of the Chicago History Museum
Page 133   © Wernher Krutein/Photovault
Page 134   Image (DN-0080464) courtesy of the Chicago History Museum
Page 135   © Wernher Krutein/Photovault
Page 136   Image (DN-0081447) courtesy of the Chicago History Museum
Page 137   © Wernher Krutein/Photovault
Page 138   © G.E. Kidder Smith/CORBIS
Page 139   © Wernher Krutein/Photovault
Page 140   Image (DN-0007162) courtesy of the Chicago History Museum
Page 141   © Wernher Krutein/Photovault

Index